Graphic Medieval History

REBELLION AND REVOLT

By Gary Jeffrey & Illustrated by Terry Riley

Crabtree Publishing Company
www.crabtreebooks.com

Crabtree Publishing Company
www.crabtreebooks.com
1-800-387-7650

Publishing in Canada
616 Welland Ave.
St. Catharines, ON
L2M 5V6

Published in the United States
PMB 59051, 350 Fifth Ave.
59th Floor,
New York, NY 10118

Published in **2014 by CRABTREE PUBLISHING COMPANY.**

Printed in Canada/032014/MA20140124

Created and produced by:

David West Children's Books

Project development, design, and concept:

David West Children's Books

Author and designer: Gary Jeffrey

Illustrator: Terry Riley

Editor: Kathy Middleton

Proofreader: Adrianna Morganelli

Production coordinator and

Prepress technician:

Ken Wright

Print coordinator:

Margaret Amy Salter

Photo credits:

p47, xlibber

Library and Archives Canada Cataloguing in Publication

Jeffrey, Gary, author
    Rebellion and revolt / Gary Jeffrey ; illustrator: Terry Riley.

(Graphic medieval history)
Includes index.
Issued in print and electronic formats.
ISBN 978-0-7787-0399-0 (bound).--ISBN 978-0-7787-0405-8 (pbk.).--ISBN 978-1-4271-7511-3 (html).--ISBN 978-1-4271-7517-5 (pdf)

    1. Scotland--History--Wallace's Rising, 1297-1304--Juvenile literature. 2. Tyler's Insurrection, 1381--Juvenile literature. 3. Glendower, Owen, approximately 1354-1416--Juvenile literature. 4. Scotland--History--Wallace's Rising, 1297-1304--Comic books, strips, etc. 5. Tyler's Insurrection, 1381--Comic books, strips, etc. 6. Glendower, Owen, approximately 1354-1416--Comic books, strips, etc. 7. Graphic novels. I. Riley, Terry, illustrator II. Title. III. Series: Jeffrey, Gary. Graphic medieval history.

DA176.J45 2014   j941.03   C2014-900363-3
                                        C2014-900364-1

Library of Congress Cataloging-in-Publication Data

Jeffrey, Gary.
  Rebellion and revolt / by Gary Jeffrey ; illustrated by Terry Riley.
      pages cm. -- (Graphic medieval history)
  Includes index.
  ISBN 978-0-7787-0399-0 (reinforced library binding : alkaline paper) -- ISBN 978-0-7787-0405-8 (paperback : alkaline paper) -- ISBN 978-1-4271-7511-3 (electronic html) -- ISBN 978-1-4271-7517-5 (electronic pdf)
  1. Peasant uprisings--Great Britain--History--To 1500--Juvenile literature. 2. Peasant uprisings--Great Britain--History--To 1500--Comic books, strips, etc. 3. Great Britain--History--Medieval period, 1066-1485--Juvenile literature. 4. Great Britain--History--Medieval period, 1066-1485--Comic books, strips, etc. 5. Peasants--England--History--To 1500--Juvenile literature. 6. Peasants--England--History--To 1500--Comic books, strips, etc. 7. England--Social conditions--1066-1485--Juvenile literature. 8. England--Social conditions--1066-1485--Comic books, strips, etc. 9. Graphic novels. I. Riley, Terry, illustrator. II. Title.

DA235.J44 2014
 941.03--dc23

                                  2014002261

Contents

Wars of Independence

The medieval kingdom of Alba (Scotland) was established in the 9th century. Its people were descended from the Picts, who were Celts who had kept themselves separated from the Roman invaders and Saxon settlers who had colonized England. Scotland was ruled by a succession of kings until Alexander III died in 1286—leaving no heir to the throne.

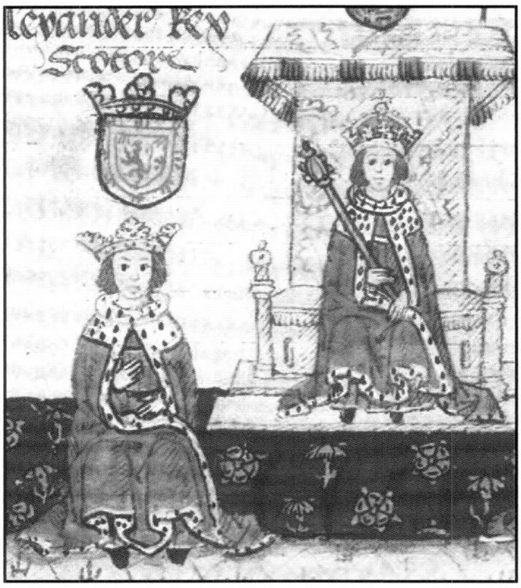

King Alexander III (left) visits Edward I, the English king who saw the succession crisis as a way to stake his claim on Scottish rule.

The Great Cause

Alexander's granddaughter, Margaret, Princess of Norway, was declared the heir at three years old, causing a quarrel among Scottish nobles who each wanted to seize the crown. The English king, Edward I, arranged for Margaret to marry his son Edward, Prince of Wales. That way Edward would become king of both England and Scotland.

But Margaret died on the way to Scotland. The Scottish nobles again pushed their own claims. To avoid civil war (and become overlord of Scotland himself), Edward I agreed to judge who had the strongest claim. He chose John Balliol, who was crowned in 1292.

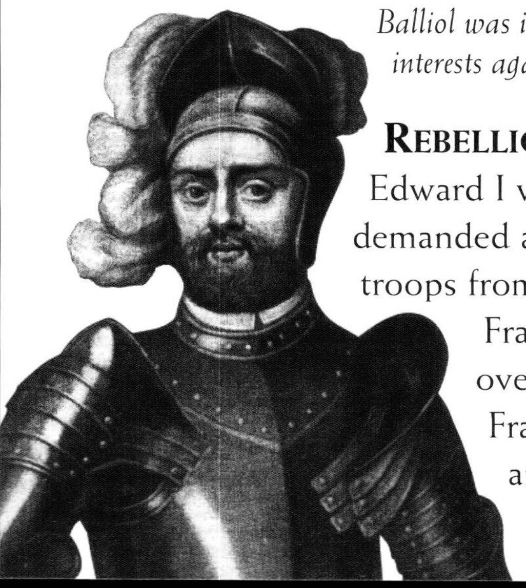

Balliol was in a weak position and failed to protect Scottish interests against King Edward I's ruthless demands.

Rebellion!

Edward I was now Lord Paramount of Scotland. He demanded a promise of loyalty and a contribution of troops from the Scottish nobles to aid his war against France. Balliol's subjects objected. The nobles overruled Balliol and made a treaty with France instead. Furious, Edward I gathered an army to invade the rebellious state.

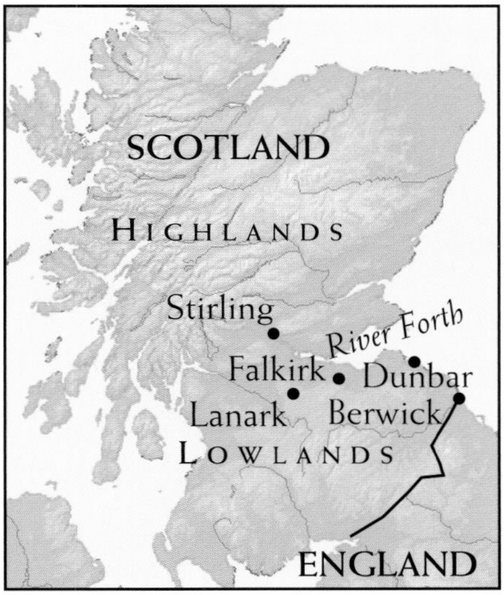
SCOTLAND
HIGHLANDS
Stirling
River Forth
Falkirk
Dunbar
Lanark
Berwick
LOWLANDS
ENGLAND

Invasion of Scotland!

On the border between England and Scotland, English forces sacked the town of Berwick in 1296. Ten thousand men, women, and children were slain. Then a force of English knights went to Dunbar, where Scots held the castle. Balliol sent his knights to defend it, but they were outsmarted and captured by the English.

The River Forth divides the Scottish highlands and lowlands. A bridge crosses the river at Stirling.

A Scottish Leader Rises

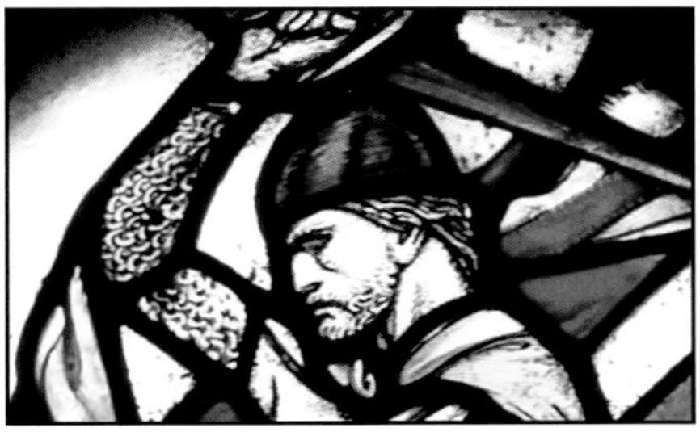

Wallace features on a Scottish stained glass window.

The short war was won, and the English took over the Scottish lowlands. Then, in May 1297, an English sheriff was assassinated in Lanark by a minor Scottish noble, a rebel named William Wallace. Balliol had already abdicated and his remaining nobles had pledged their loyalty to Edward, but small rebellions kept breaking out in Scotland. Wallace had military expertise and quickly rose to become leader of an organized commoners' army, alongside Andrew Moray, a Scottish knight who wanted independence for Scotland.

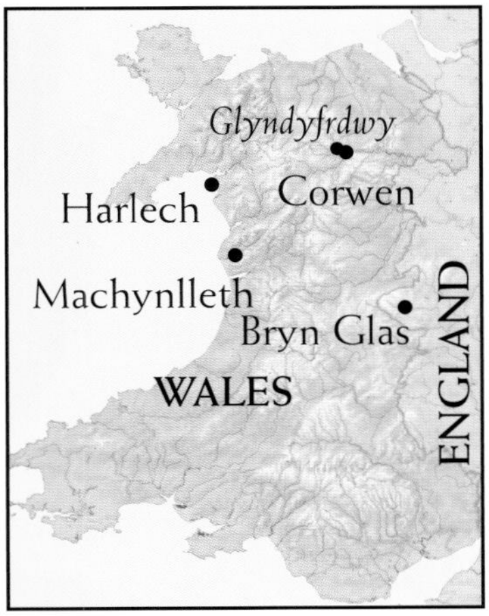
Glyndyfrdwy
Harlech
Corwen
Machynlleth
Bryn Glas
WALES
ENGLAND

Owain Glyndwr was Lord of Glyndyfrdwy, Denbighshire.

Uprisings in Wales

In Wales, Edward I had defeated a series of rebellions staged by the Prince of Wales, Llywelyn ap Gruffydd, years earlier. A line of English kings would dominate Wales for the next hundred years until 1399 when England's Richard II was overthrown by Henry IV. Under the new reign, an English landowner in Wales named Reynold de Grey felt entitled to steal land from his neighbor, Owain Glyndwr, as well as brand him a traitor to the crown. The Welsh noble had no choice but to rebel.

Peasants' Revolt

John of Gaunt, the first Duke of Lancaster, was hated by the commoners.

In 1377, Richard II became king of England at age ten. His grandfather, King Edward III, had ruled for 50 years. Richard's father had died a year earlier, so the crown passed to Richard. A council of advisors would rule until he came of age. The lower classes supported Richard but were unhappy about the way the country was being governed.

SEEDS OF DISCORD

The Black Death of 1348 and other plagues had killed many laborers. Lords now had a much smaller pool of workers to choose from. A good tenant was more valuable than ever before, so labor wages increased. The war with France had become a series of costly failures, most of them headed by John of Gaunt, Richard's uncle.

John of Gaunt forced the government to put in place three poll taxes which would pay for the war out of the pockets of the lower classes. The last of these taxes was so high it caused revolts to break out, first in Essex, then in Kent, both led by an ex-soldier named Wat Tyler.

The "mad priest of Kent," John Ball, stirred up commoners who formed a rebel army. Ball preached to them about freedom and equality, giving the peasant soldiers a righteous cause for revolution.

COMMONERS MARCH

Mobs from Kent, Essex, Norfolk, and Suffolk marched on London shouting, "With King Richard and the true commons of England!" Their targets were the members of the hated King's Council and their properties, but especially John of Gaunt. The rebels crossed London Bridge and began to attack palaces and institutions within the walled city. Richard II hurried to the safety of the Tower of London. But the king's main army was in the north with his uncle, in case of an invasion by the Scots. Richard decided to negotiate with the rebels.

John of Gaunt's Savoy Palace, the finest in London, was set on fire by the mob. The huge mansion was reduced to a burned-out shell in three days.

When Richard traveled to negotiate with the rebels, they stormed the Tower of London.

REBEL JUSTICE

At the Tower, the rebels executed the treasurer, Sir Robert Hales, and Archbishop Sudbury, who was blamed for the third poll tax. Then they went on a three-day rampage, burning, looting, and murdering. To Richard it seemed as though the city was doomed...

The Battle of Stirling Bridge
The First Scottish War of Independence

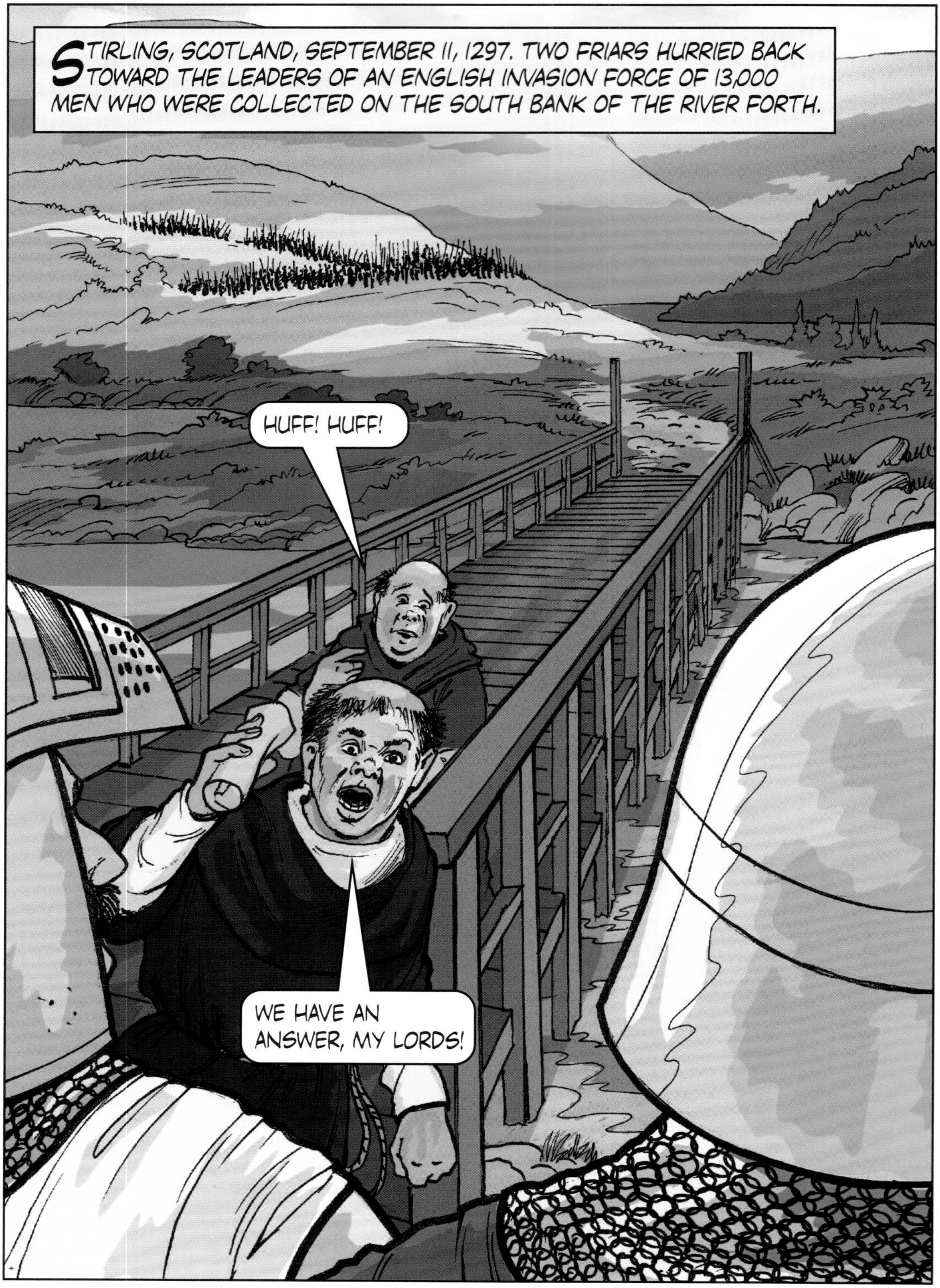
STIRLING, SCOTLAND, SEPTEMBER 11, 1297. TWO FRIARS HURRIED BACK TOWARD THE LEADERS OF AN ENGLISH INVASION FORCE OF 13,000 MEN WHO WERE COLLECTED ON THE SOUTH BANK OF THE RIVER FORTH.
HUFF! HUFF!
WE HAVE AN ANSWER, MY LORDS!

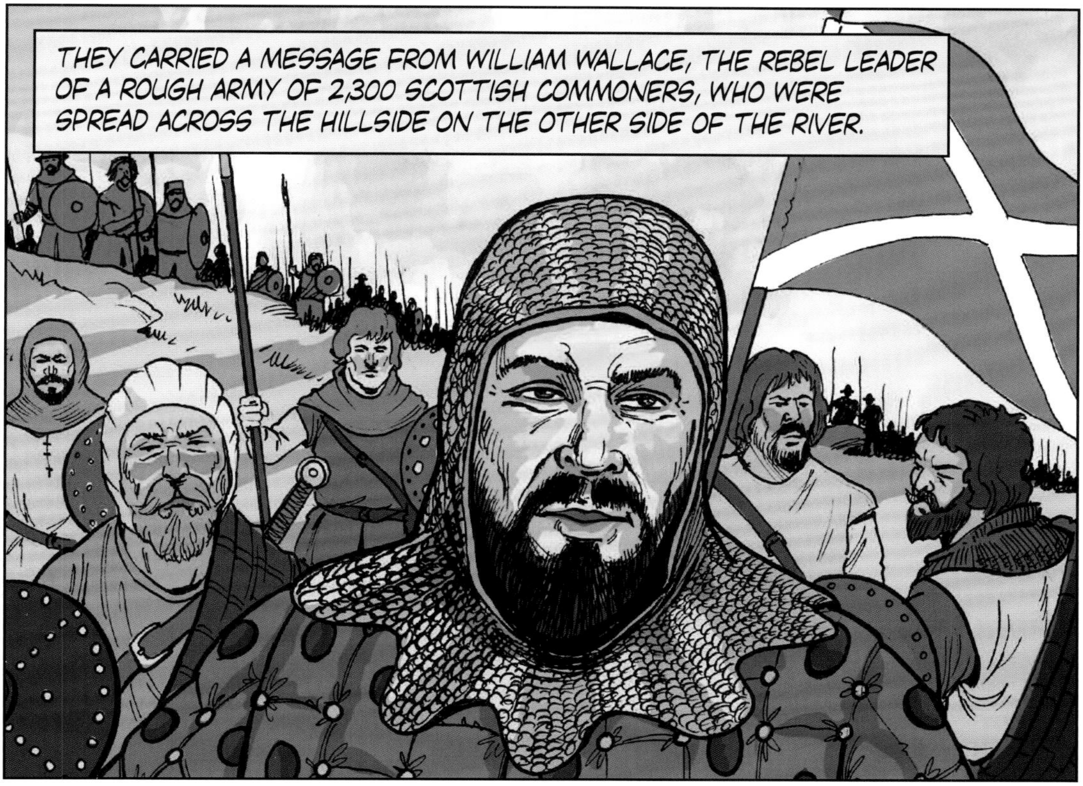
THEY CARRIED A MESSAGE FROM WILLIAM WALLACE, THE REBEL LEADER OF A ROUGH ARMY OF 2,300 SCOTTISH COMMONERS, WHO WERE SPREAD ACROSS THE HILLSIDE ON THE OTHER SIDE OF THE RIVER.

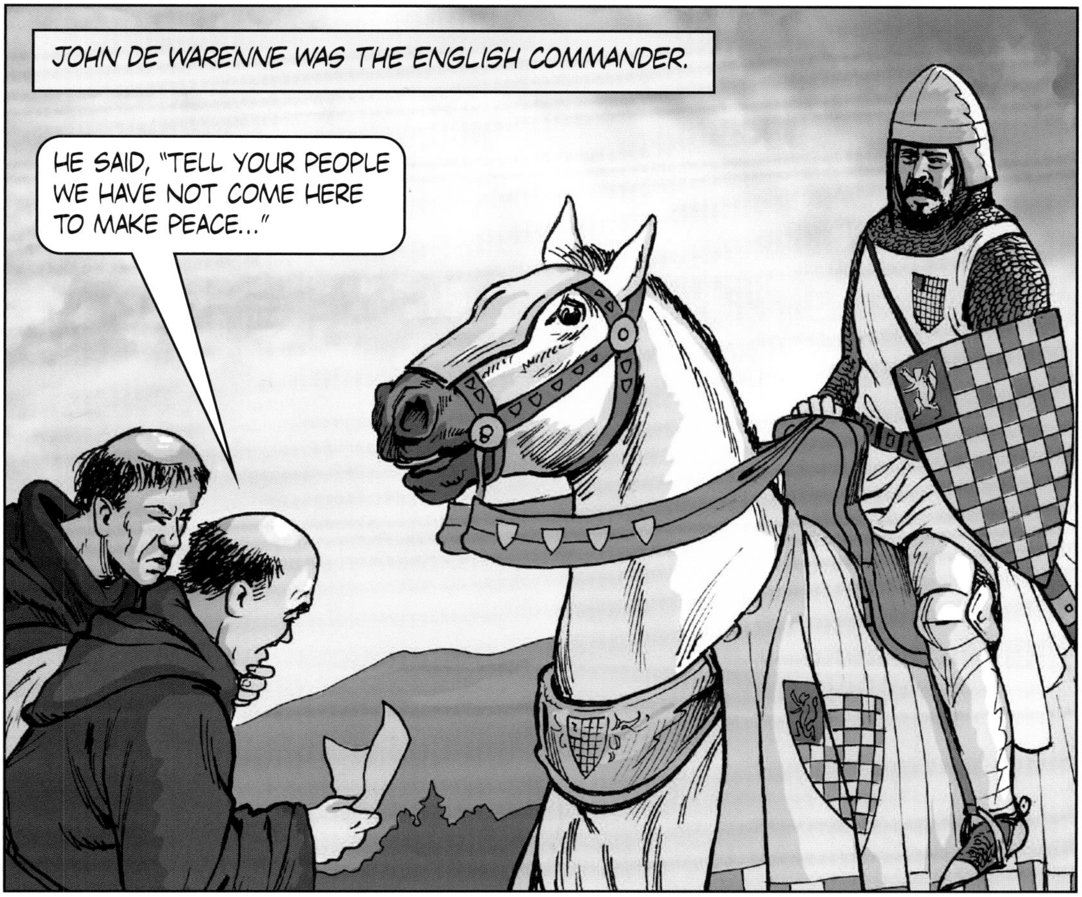
JOHN DE WARENNE WAS THE ENGLISH COMMANDER.
HE SAID, "TELL YOUR PEOPLE WE HAVE NOT COME HERE TO MAKE PEACE..."

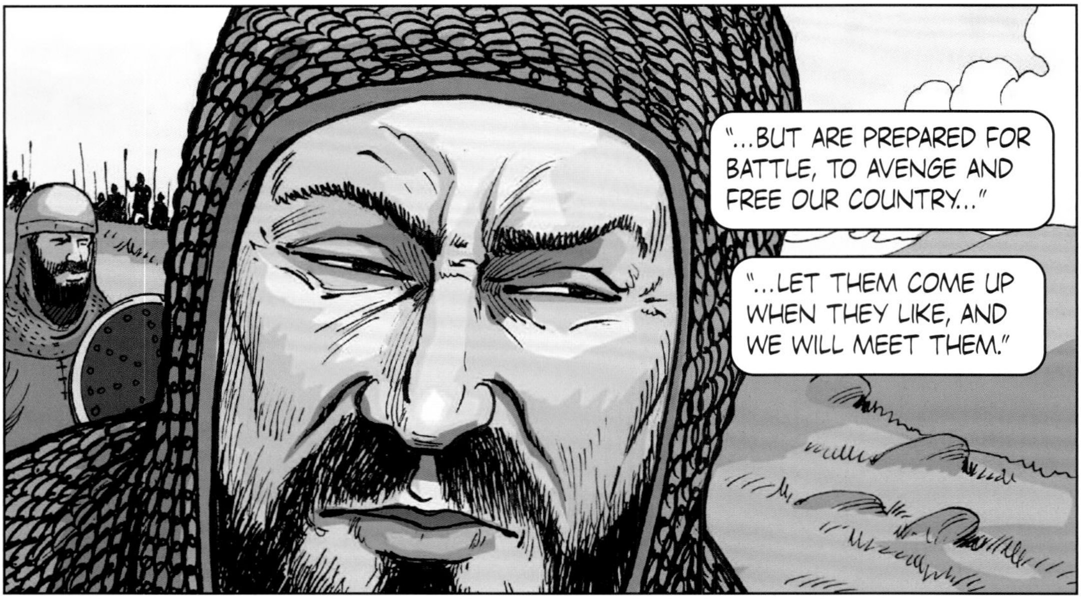
"...BUT ARE PREPARED FOR BATTLE, TO AVENGE AND FREE OUR COUNTRY..."
"...LET THEM COME UP WHEN THEY LIKE, AND WE WILL MEET THEM."

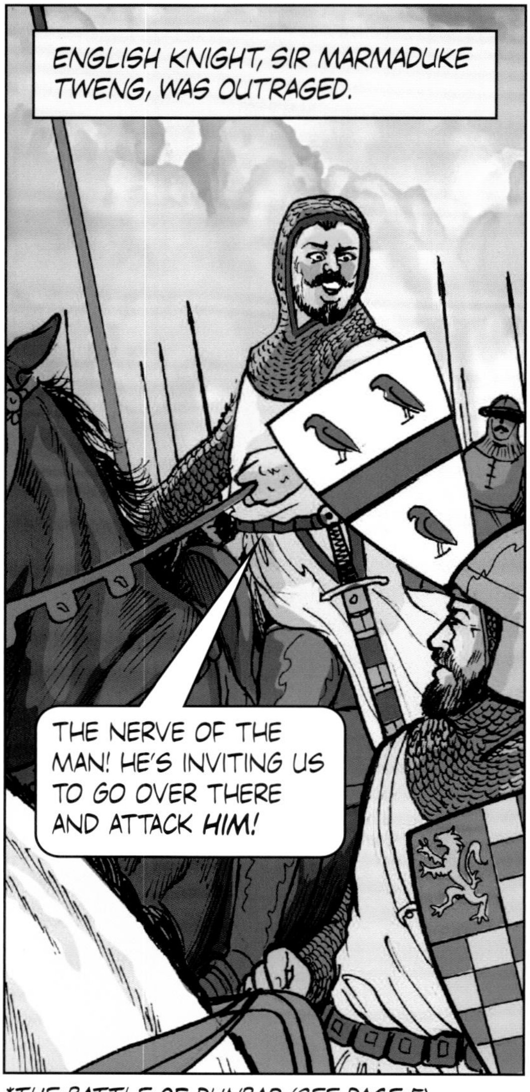
ENGLISH KNIGHT, SIR MARMADUKE TWENG, WAS OUTRAGED.
THE NERVE OF THE MAN! HE'S INVITING US TO GO OVER THERE AND ATTACK HIM!

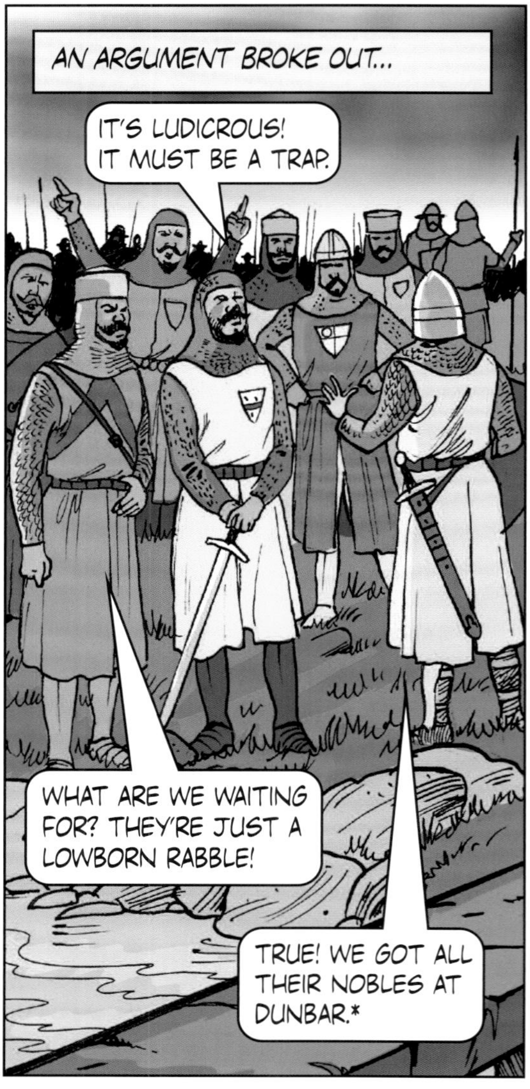
AN ARGUMENT BROKE OUT...
IT'S LUDICROUS! IT MUST BE A TRAP.
WHAT ARE WE WAITING FOR? THEY'RE JUST A LOWBORN RABBLE!
TRUE! WE GOT ALL THEIR NOBLES AT DUNBAR.*

*THE BATTLE OF DUNBAR (SEE PAGE 5).

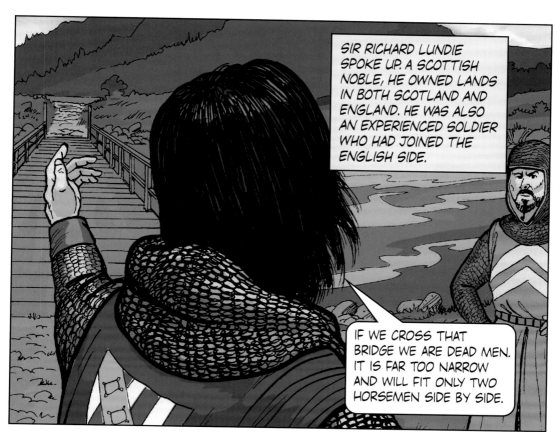

SIR RICHARD LUNDIE SPOKE UP. A SCOTTISH NOBLE, HE OWNED LANDS IN BOTH SCOTLAND AND ENGLAND. HE WAS ALSO AN EXPERIENCED SOLDIER WHO HAD JOINED THE ENGLISH SIDE.

IF WE CROSS THAT BRIDGE WE ARE DEAD MEN. IT IS FAR TOO NARROW AND WILL FIT ONLY TWO HORSEMEN SIDE BY SIDE.

GIVE ME A CAVALRY FORCE. THERE'S A FORD JUST UP THE RIVER WHERE SIXTY KNIGHTS CAN CROSS AT THE SAME TIME...

WHY SHOULD WE TRUST HIM? HE'S A SCOT!

...AND WE CAN GET IN BEHIND AND TAKE THEM BY SURPRISE...

HURRUMPH!

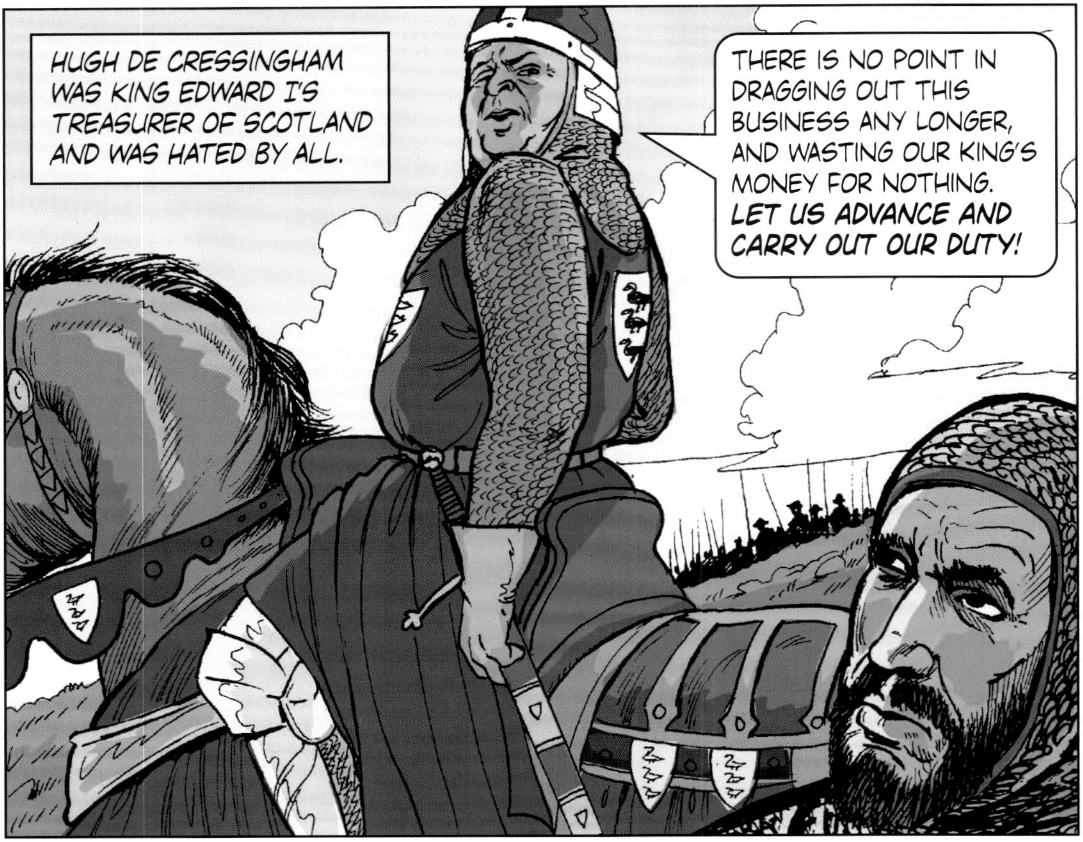
HUGH DE CRESSINGHAM WAS KING EDWARD I'S TREASURER OF SCOTLAND AND WAS HATED BY ALL.
THERE IS NO POINT IN DRAGGING OUT THIS BUSINESS ANY LONGER, AND WASTING OUR KING'S MONEY FOR NOTHING. LET US ADVANCE AND CARRY OUT OUR DUTY!

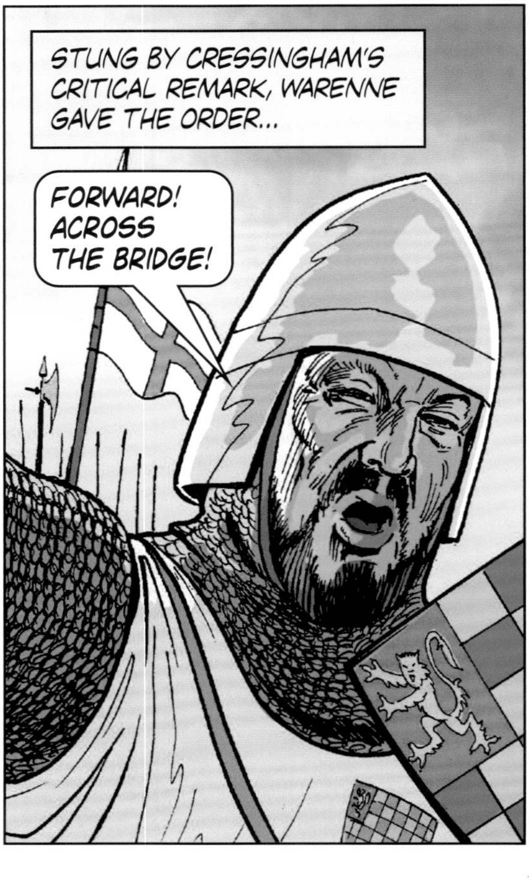
STUNG BY CRESSINGHAM'S CRITICAL REMARK, WARENNE GAVE THE ORDER...
FORWARD! ACROSS THE BRIDGE!

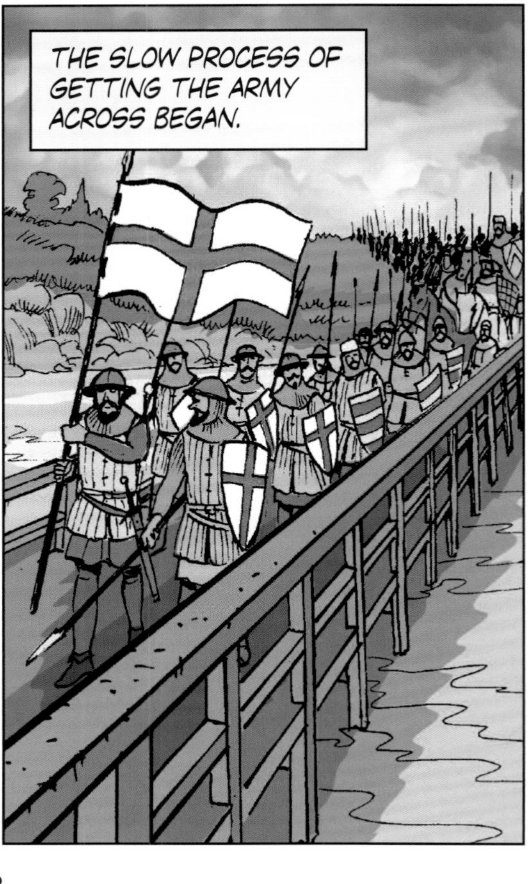
THE SLOW PROCESS OF GETTING THE ARMY ACROSS BEGAN.

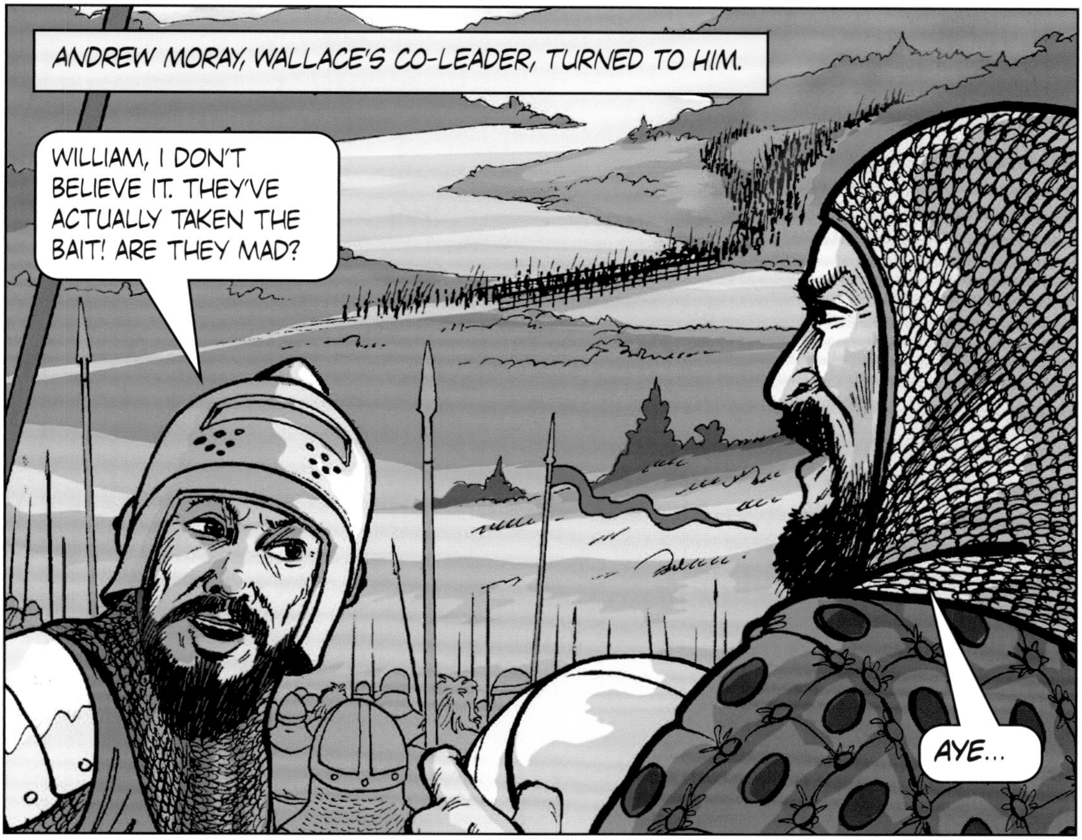
ANDREW MORAY, WALLACE'S CO-LEADER, TURNED TO HIM.
WILLIAM, I DON'T BELIEVE IT. THEY'VE ACTUALLY TAKEN THE BAIT! ARE THEY MAD?
AYE...

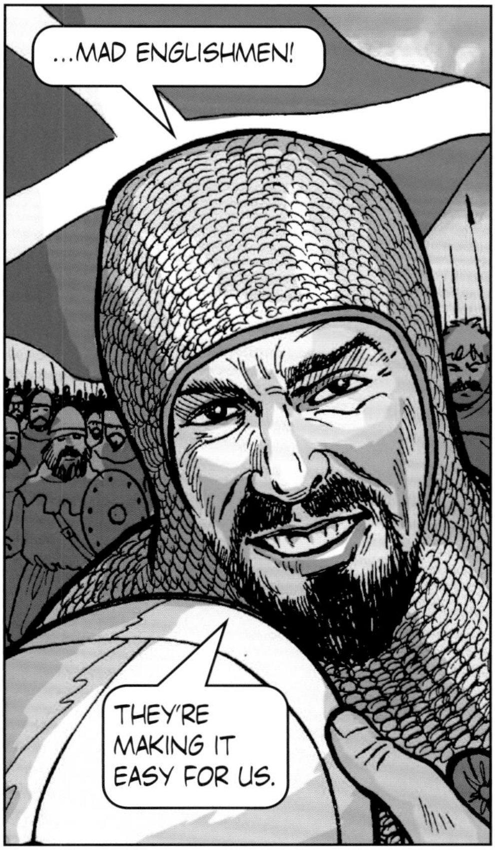
...MAD ENGLISHMEN!
THEY'RE MAKING IT EASY FOR US.

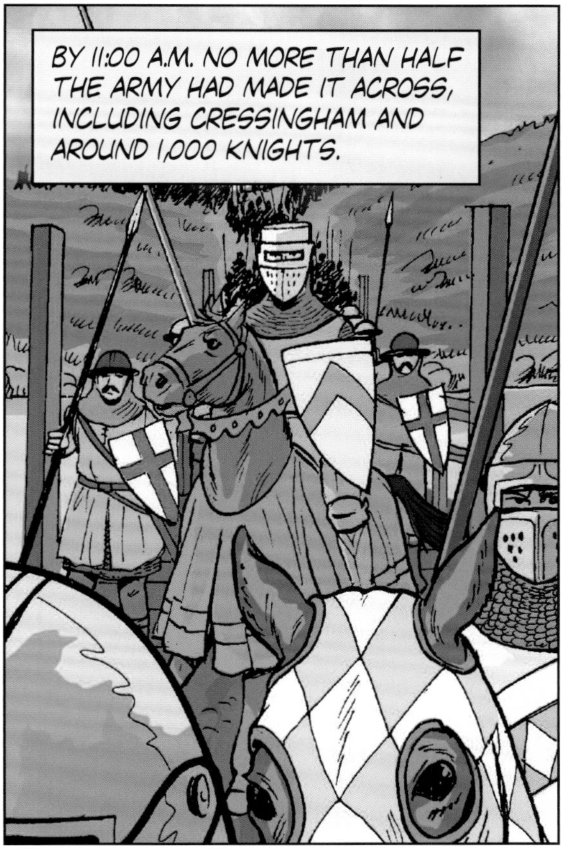
BY 11:00 A.M. NO MORE THAN HALF THE ARMY HAD MADE IT ACROSS, INCLUDING CRESSINGHAM AND AROUND 1,000 KNIGHTS.

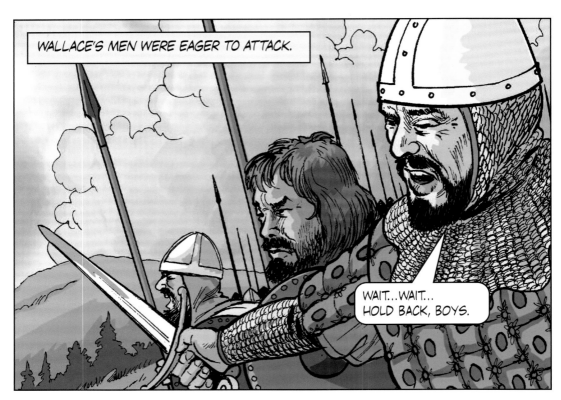

WALLACE'S MEN WERE EAGER TO ATTACK.

WAIT...WAIT... HOLD BACK, BOYS.

WE NEED TO HAVE A GOOD NUMBER ACROSS BEFORE WE STRIKE.

LEAVE TOO MANY ON THE FAR BANK AND THEY'LL GET THE BETTER OF US IN THE END.

SOON WALLACE TOOK UP A HORN AND GAVE A SHARP BLAST.

BRAAARP

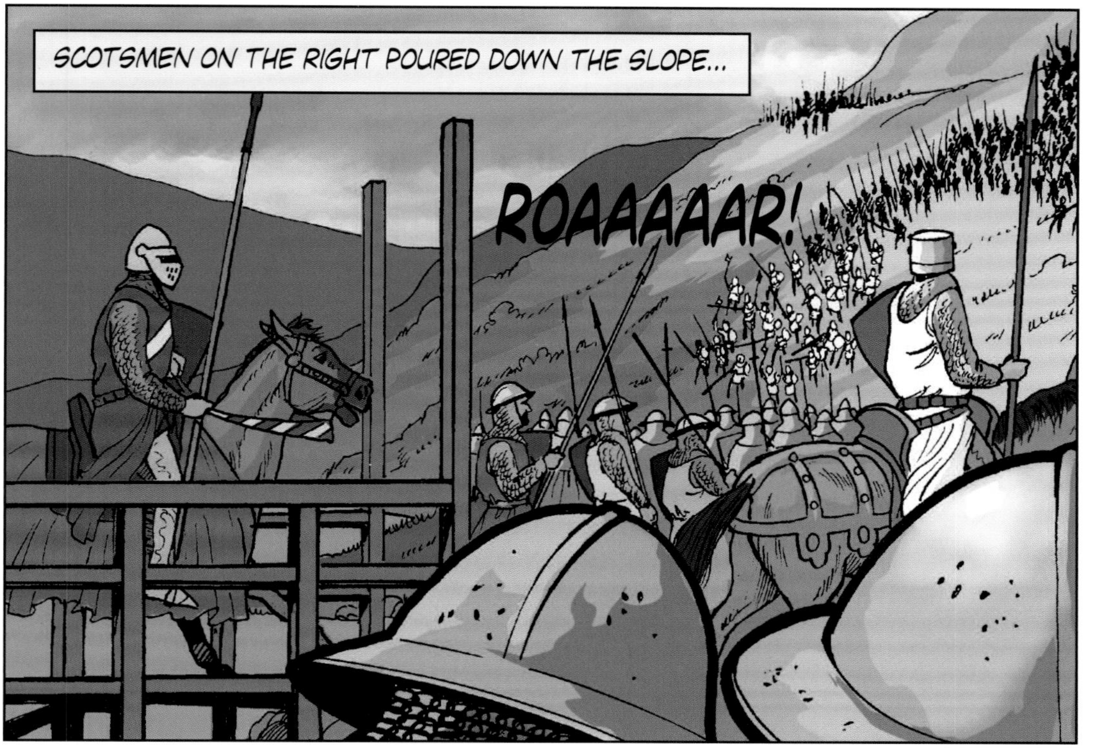
SCOTSMEN ON THE RIGHT POURED DOWN THE SLOPE...
ROAAAAAR!

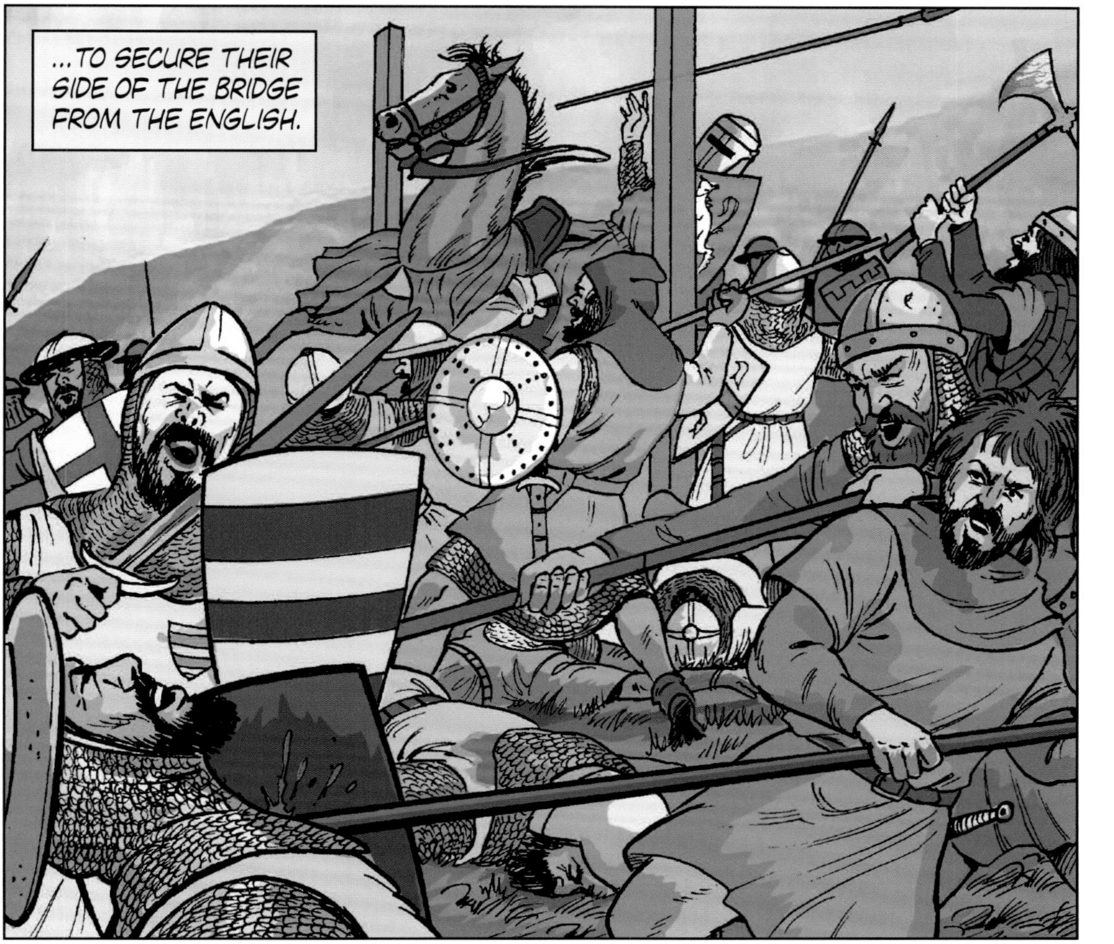
...TO SECURE THEIR SIDE OF THE BRIDGE FROM THE ENGLISH.

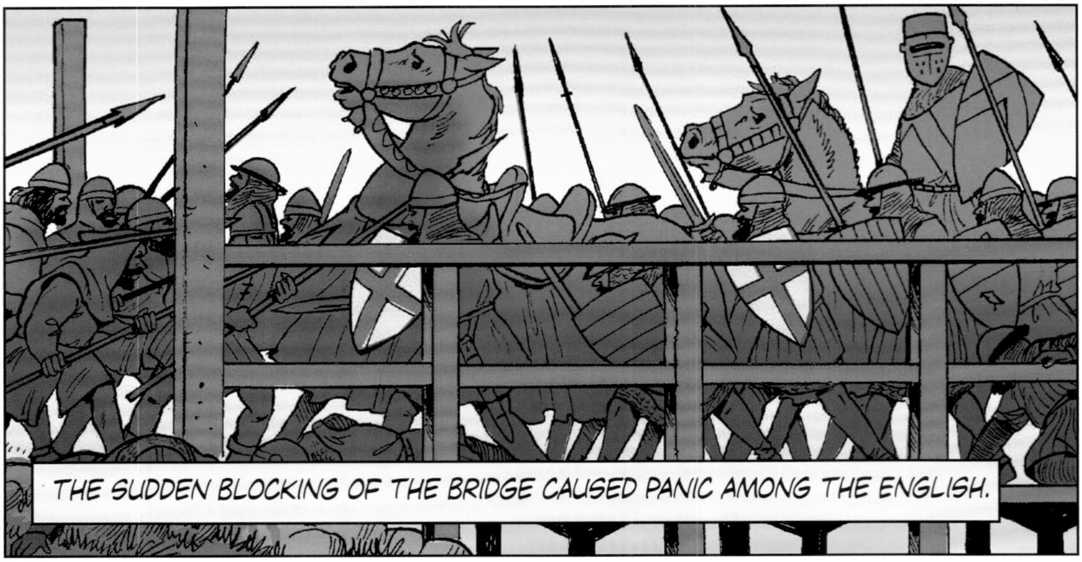
THE SUDDEN BLOCKING OF THE BRIDGE CAUSED PANIC AMONG THE ENGLISH.

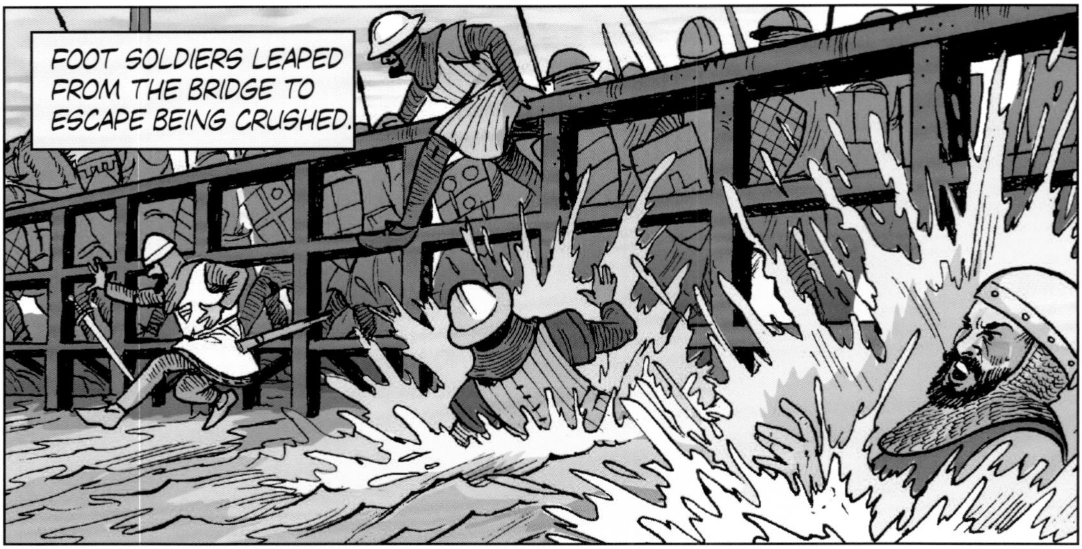
FOOT SOLDIERS LEAPED FROM THE BRIDGE TO ESCAPE BEING CRUSHED.

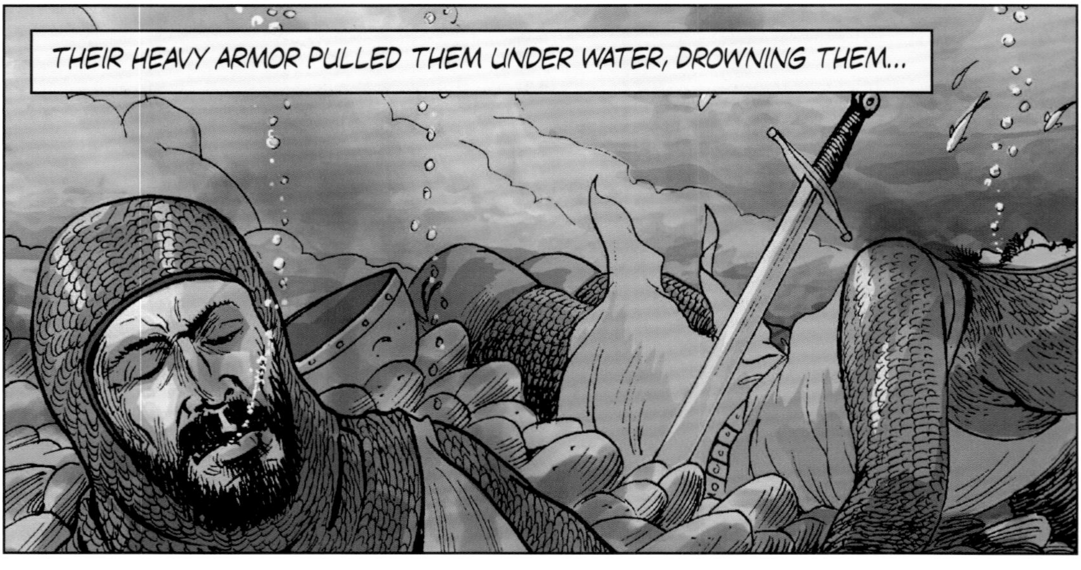
THEIR HEAVY ARMOR PULLED THEM UNDER WATER, DROWNING THEM...

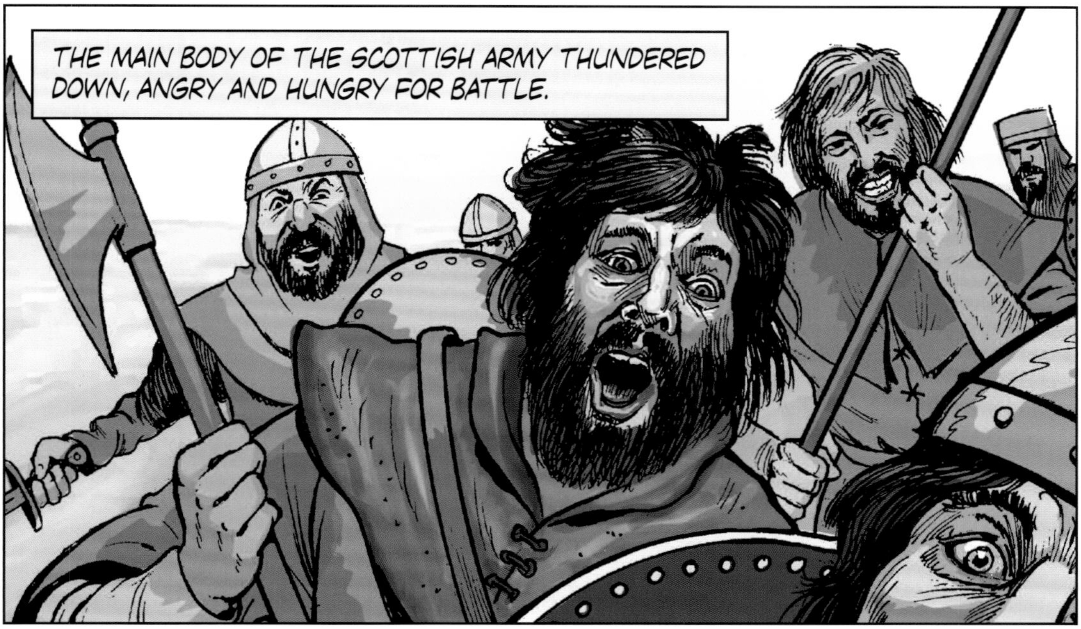
THE MAIN BODY OF THE SCOTTISH ARMY THUNDERED DOWN, ANGRY AND HUNGRY FOR BATTLE.

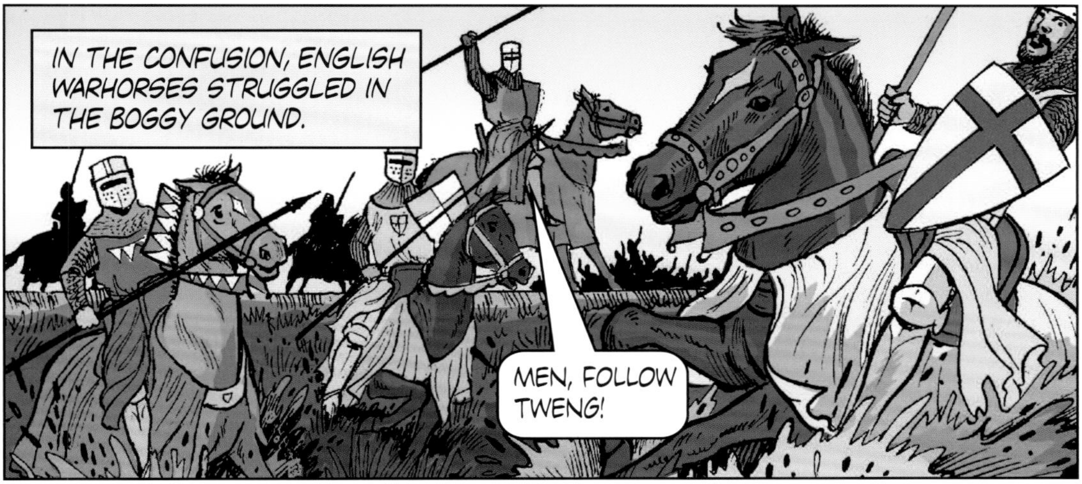
IN THE CONFUSION, ENGLISH WARHORSES STRUGGLED IN THE BOGGY GROUND.
MEN, FOLLOW TWENG!

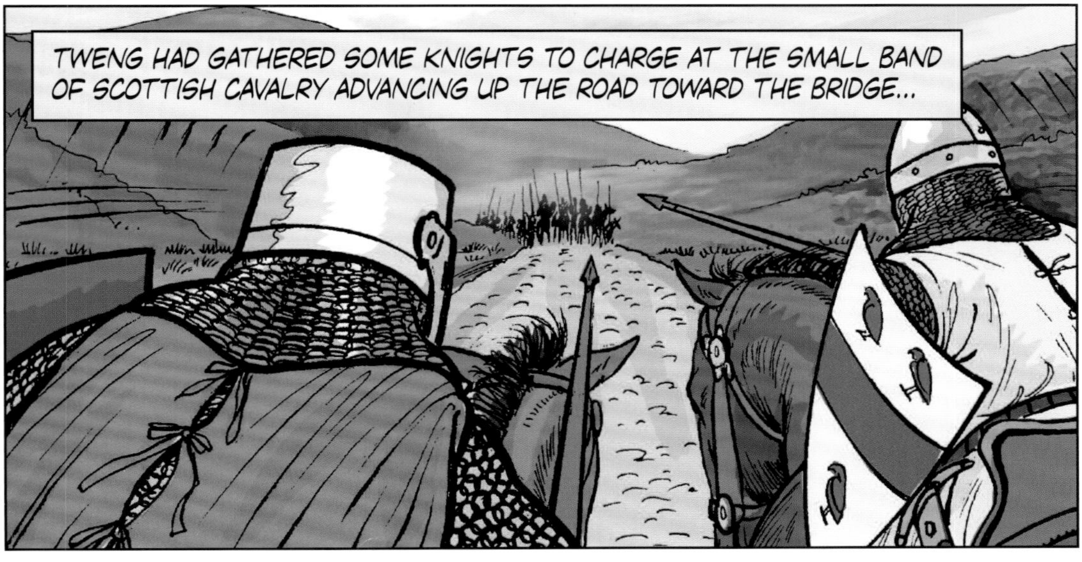
TWENG HAD GATHERED SOME KNIGHTS TO CHARGE AT THE SMALL BAND OF SCOTTISH CAVALRY ADVANCING UP THE ROAD TOWARD THE BRIDGE...

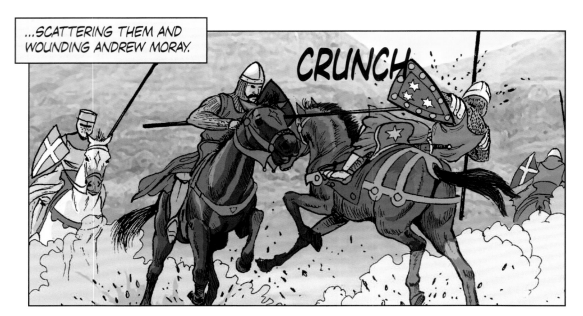

...SCATTERING THEM AND WOUNDING ANDREW MORAY.

CRUNCH

WALLACE LED HIS MEN INTO THE THICK OF THE FIGHTING.

SLICE!

CHOP!

CRESSINGHAM FELL FROM HIS HORSE...

OOHAAAR

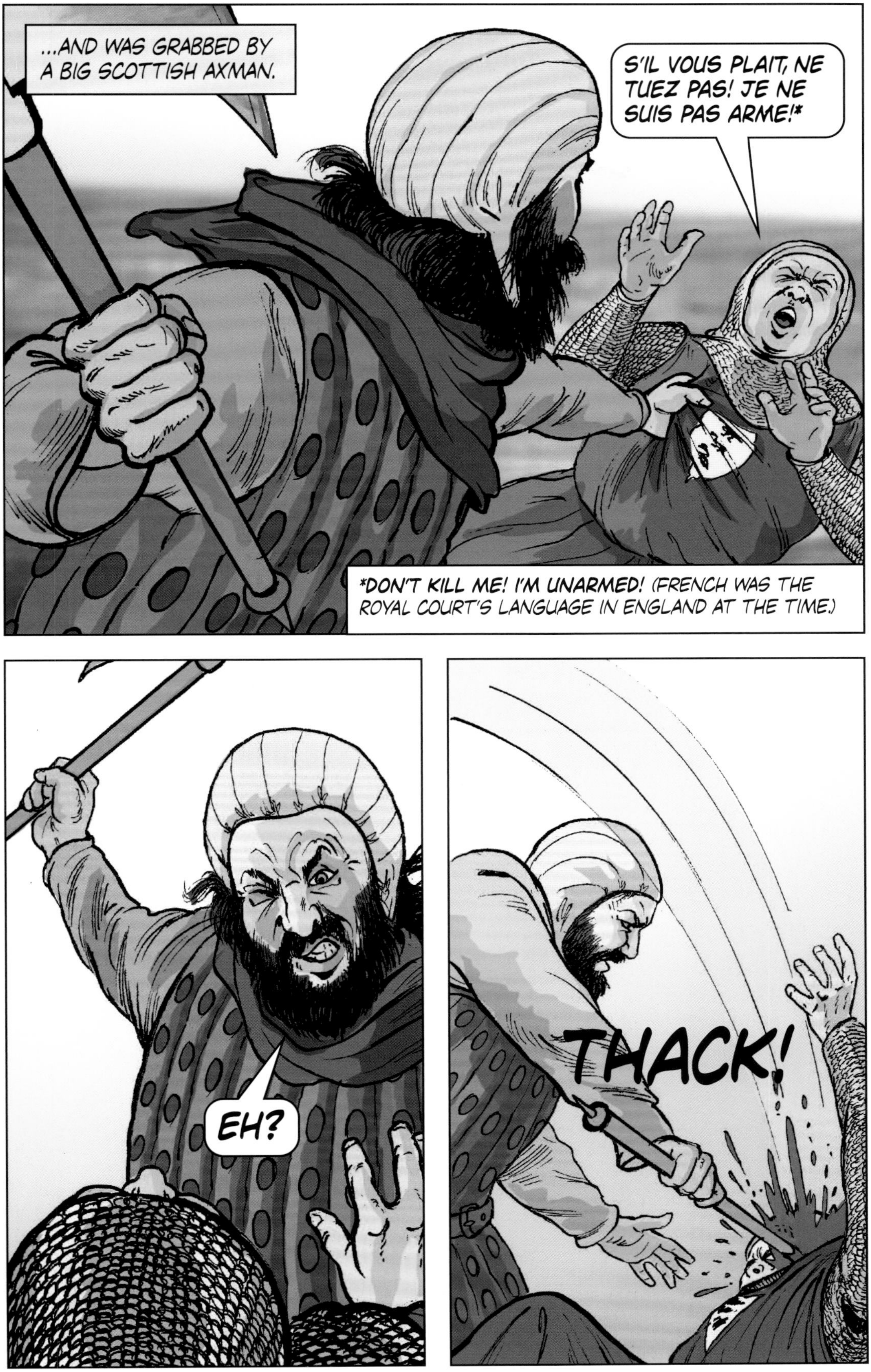
...AND WAS GRABBED BY A BIG SCOTTISH AXMAN.
S'IL VOUS PLAIT, NE TUEZ PAS! JE NE SUIS PAS ARME!*
*DON'T KILL ME! I'M UNARMED! (FRENCH WAS THE ROYAL COURT'S LANGUAGE IN ENGLAND AT THE TIME.)
EH?
THACK!

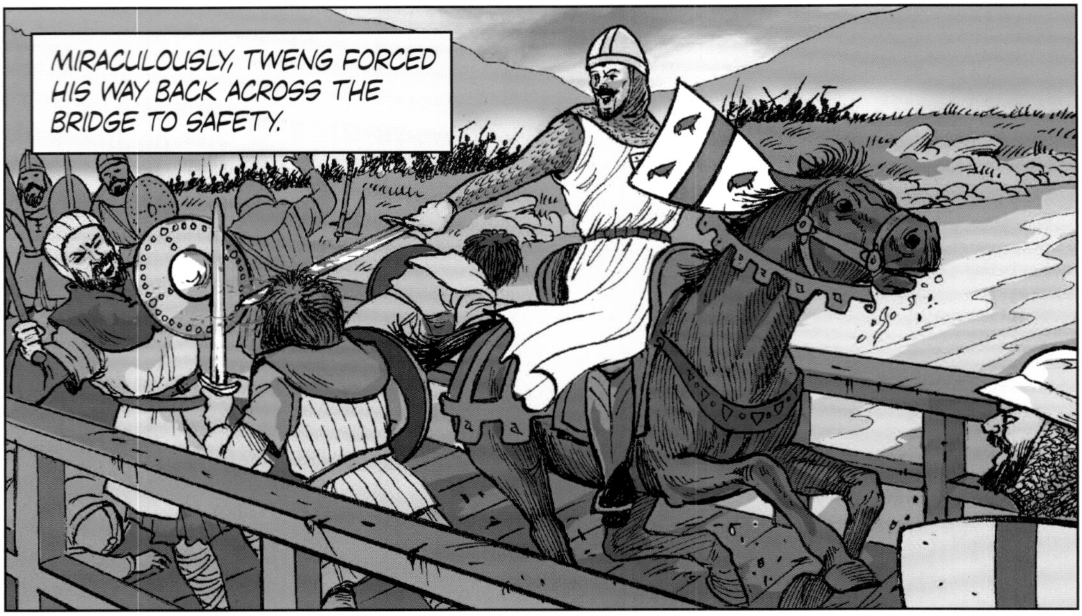
MIRACULOUSLY, TWENG FORCED HIS WAY BACK ACROSS THE BRIDGE TO SAFETY.

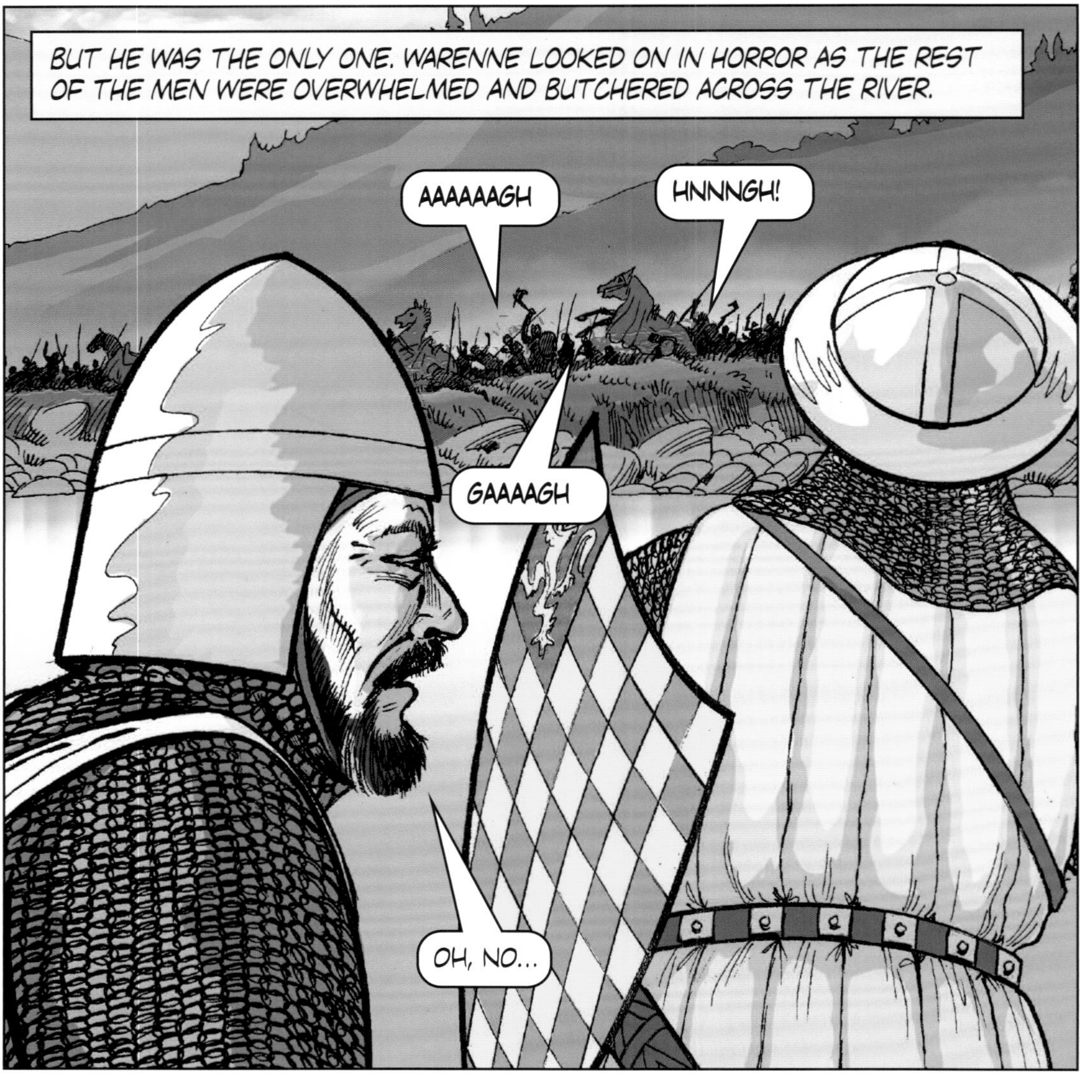
BUT HE WAS THE ONLY ONE. WARENNE LOOKED ON IN HORROR AS THE REST OF THE MEN WERE OVERWHELMED AND BUTCHERED ACROSS THE RIVER.
AAAAAAGH
HNNNGH!
GAAAAGH
OH, NO...

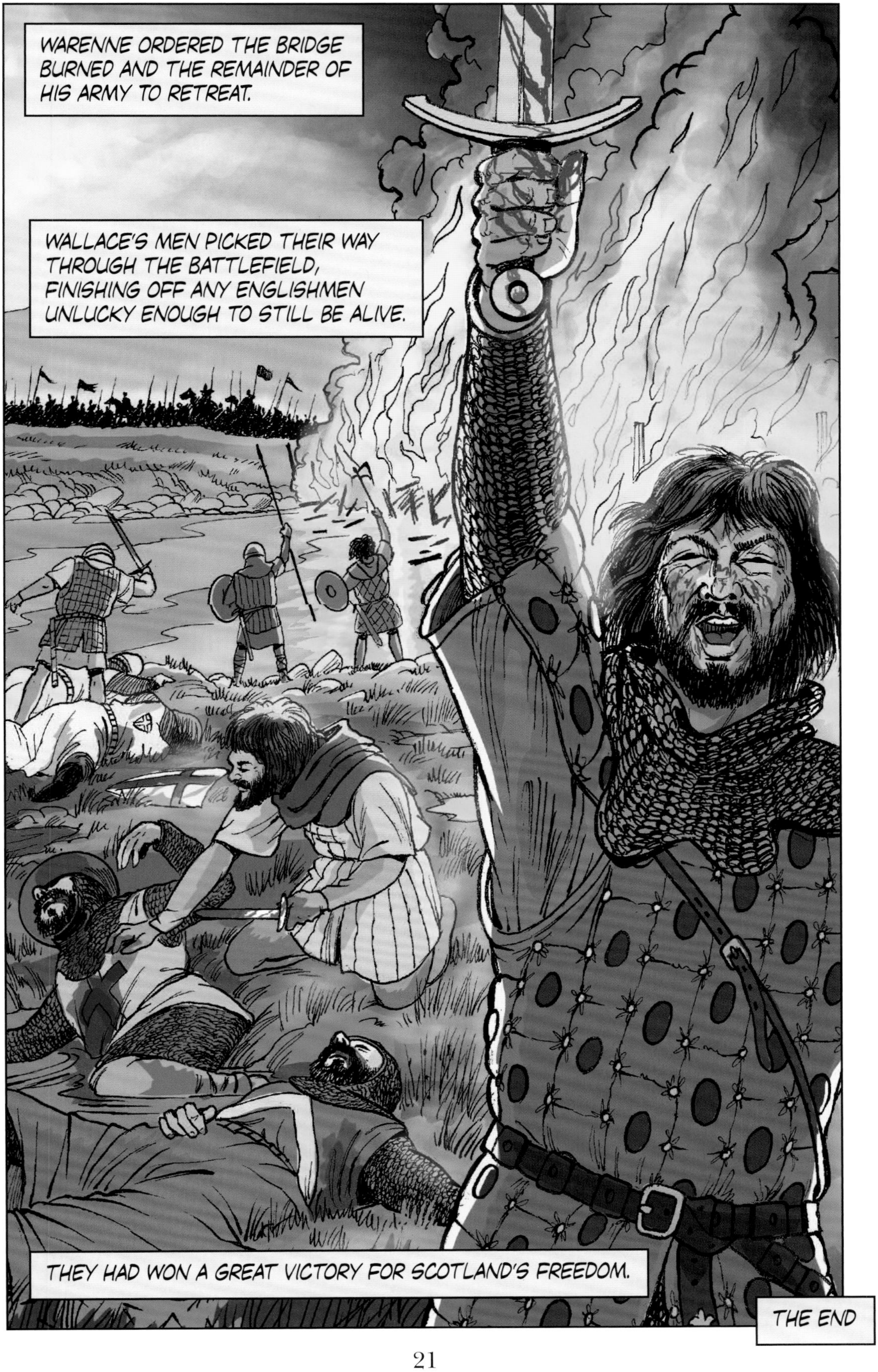
WARENNE ORDERED THE BRIDGE BURNED AND THE REMAINDER OF HIS ARMY TO RETREAT.
WALLACE'S MEN PICKED THEIR WAY THROUGH THE BATTLEFIELD, FINISHING OFF ANY ENGLISHMEN UNLUCKY ENOUGH TO STILL BE ALIVE.
THEY HAD WON A GREAT VICTORY FOR SCOTLAND'S FREEDOM.
THE END

Standoff at Smithfield
The Peasants' Revolt

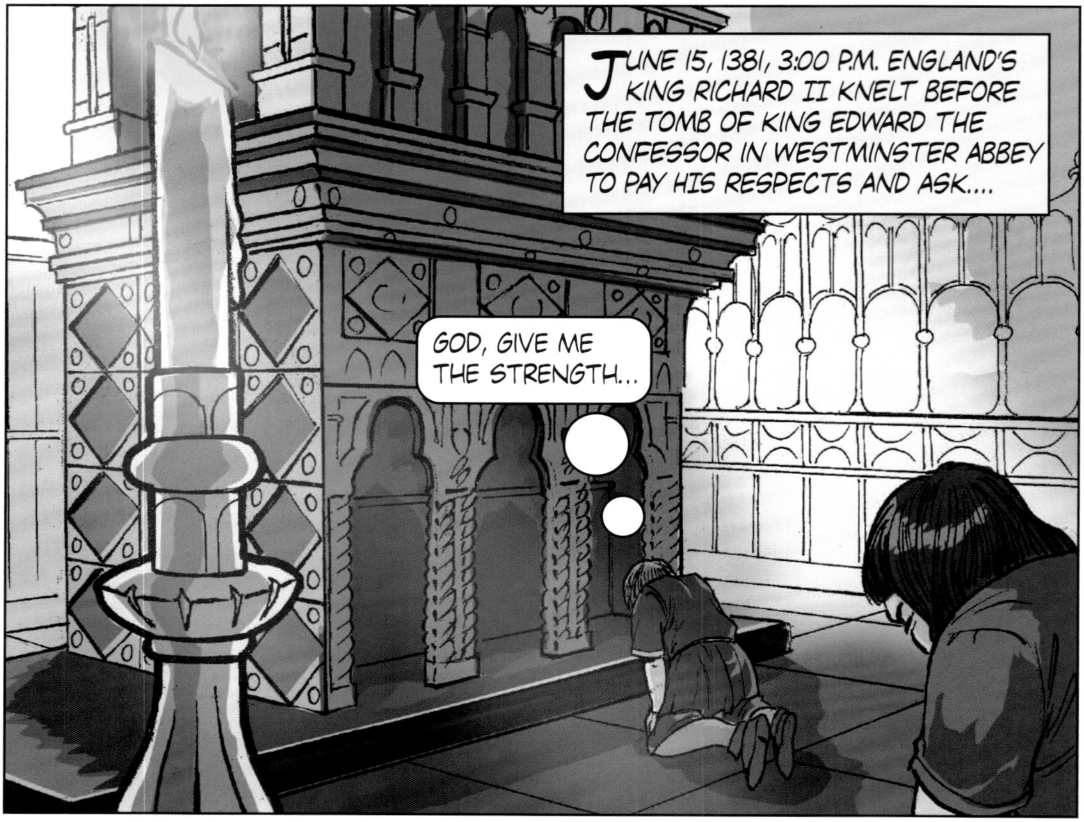
JUNE 15, 1381, 3:00 P.M. ENGLAND'S KING RICHARD II KNELT BEFORE THE TOMB OF KING EDWARD THE CONFESSOR IN WESTMINSTER ABBEY TO PAY HIS RESPECTS AND ASK....
GOD, GIVE ME THE STRENGTH...

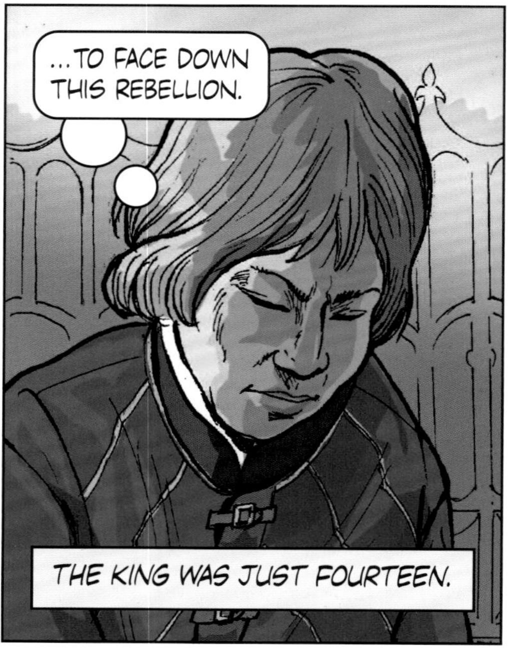
...TO FACE DOWN THIS REBELLION.
THE KING WAS JUST FOURTEEN.

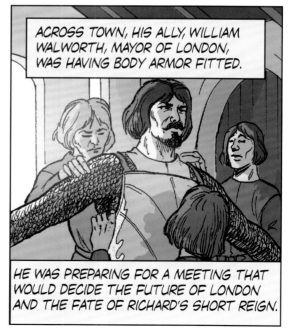

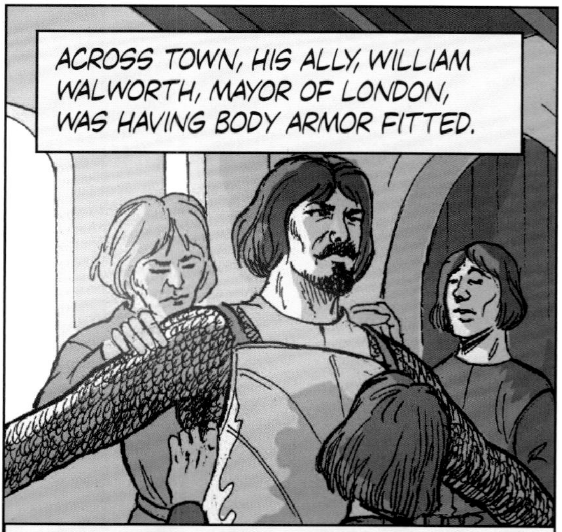
ACROSS TOWN, HIS ALLY, WILLIAM WALWORTH, MAYOR OF LONDON, WAS HAVING BODY ARMOR FITTED.
HE WAS PREPARING FOR A MEETING THAT WOULD DECIDE THE FUTURE OF LONDON AND THE FATE OF RICHARD'S SHORT REIGN.

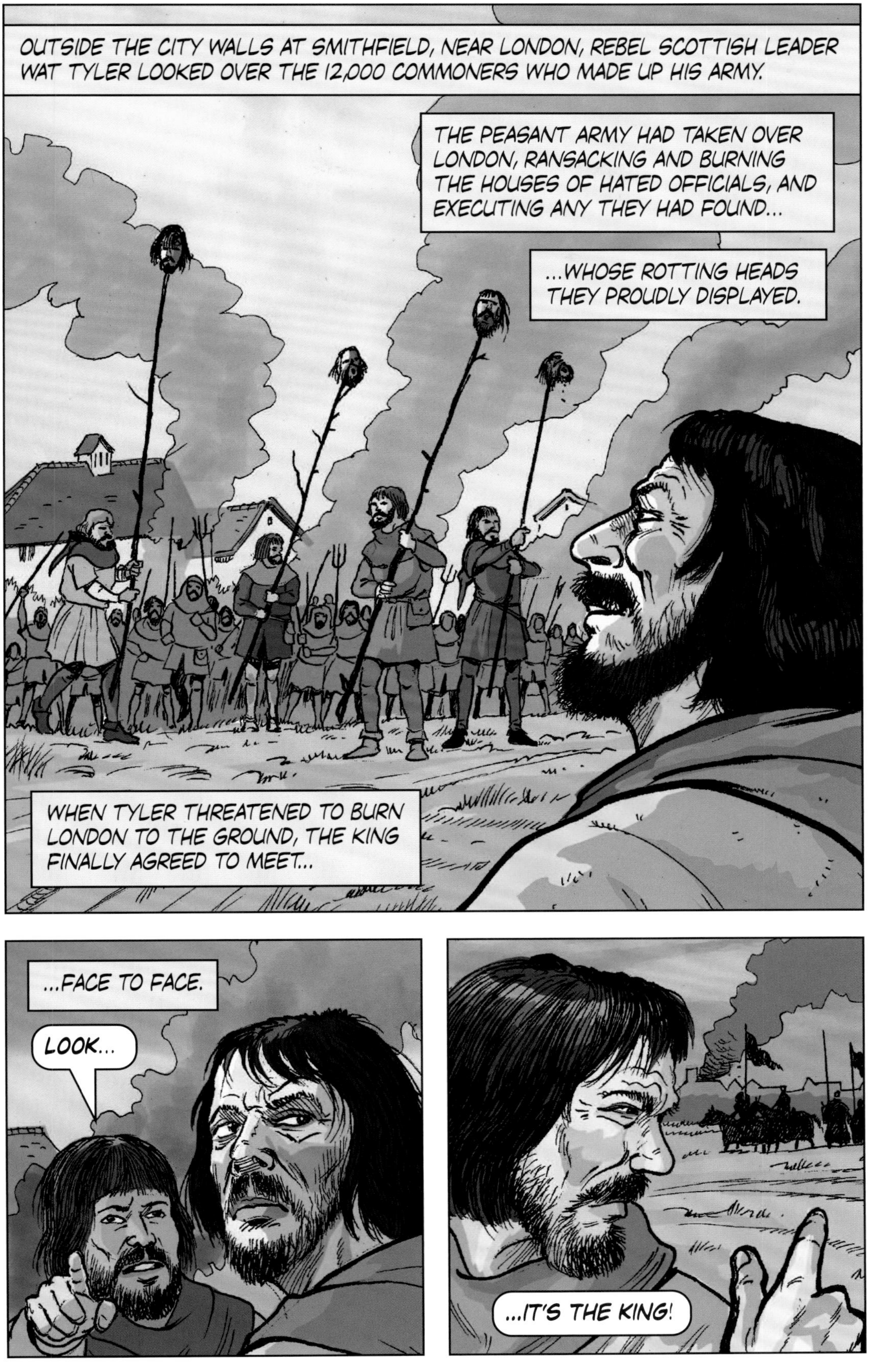
OUTSIDE THE CITY WALLS AT SMITHFIELD, NEAR LONDON, REBEL SCOTTISH LEADER WAT TYLER LOOKED OVER THE 12,000 COMMONERS WHO MADE UP HIS ARMY.
THE PEASANT ARMY HAD TAKEN OVER LONDON, RANSACKING AND BURNING THE HOUSES OF HATED OFFICIALS, AND EXECUTING ANY THEY HAD FOUND...
...WHOSE ROTTING HEADS THEY PROUDLY DISPLAYED.
WHEN TYLER THREATENED TO BURN LONDON TO THE GROUND, THE KING FINALLY AGREED TO MEET...
...FACE TO FACE.
LOOK...
...IT'S THE KING!

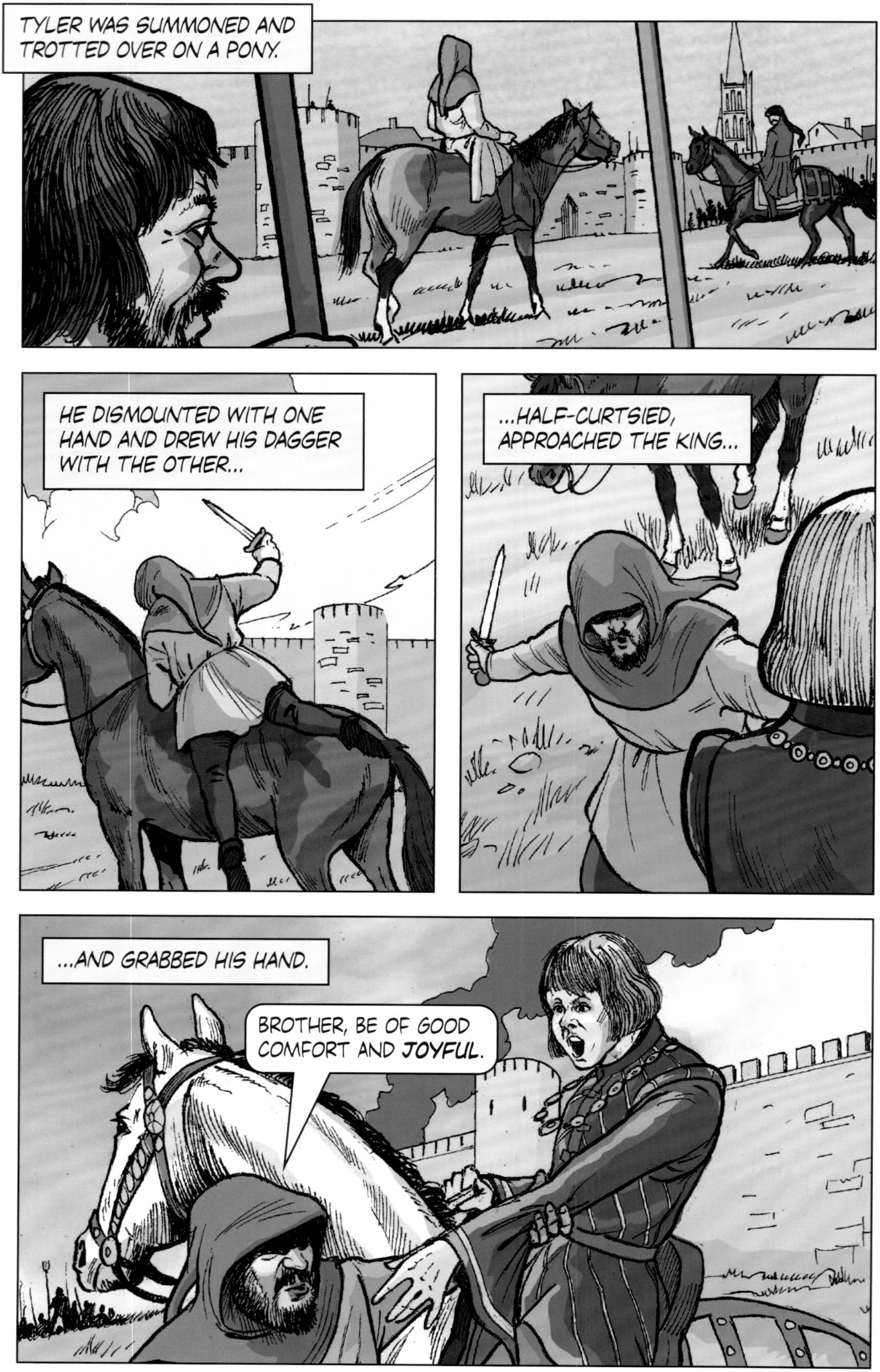
TYLER WAS SUMMONED AND TROTTED OVER ON A PONY.
HE DISMOUNTED WITH ONE HAND AND DREW HIS DAGGER WITH THE OTHER...
...HALF-CURTSIED, APPROACHED THE KING...
...AND GRABBED HIS HAND.
BROTHER, BE OF GOOD COMFORT AND JOYFUL.

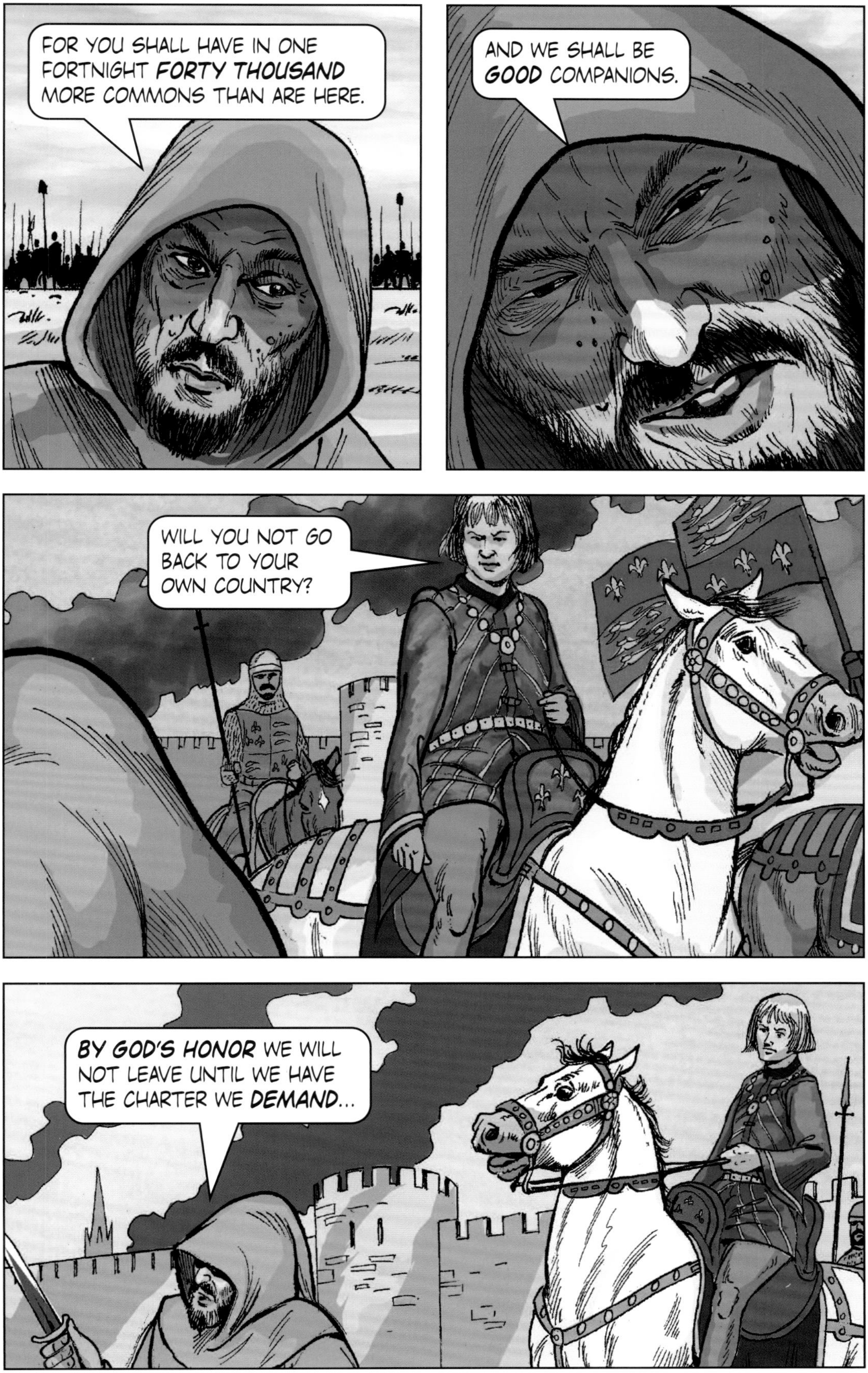
FOR YOU SHALL HAVE IN ONE FORTNIGHT **FORTY THOUSAND** MORE COMMONS THAN ARE HERE.
AND WE SHALL BE **GOOD** COMPANIONS.
WILL YOU NOT GO BACK TO YOUR OWN COUNTRY?
BY GOD'S HONOR WE WILL NOT LEAVE UNTIL WE HAVE THE CHARTER WE **DEMAND**...

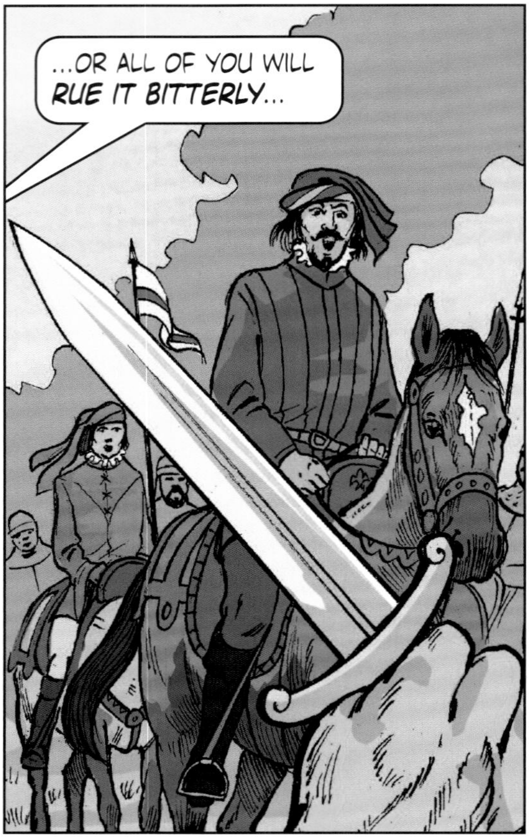
...OR ALL OF YOU WILL **RUE IT BITTERLY**...

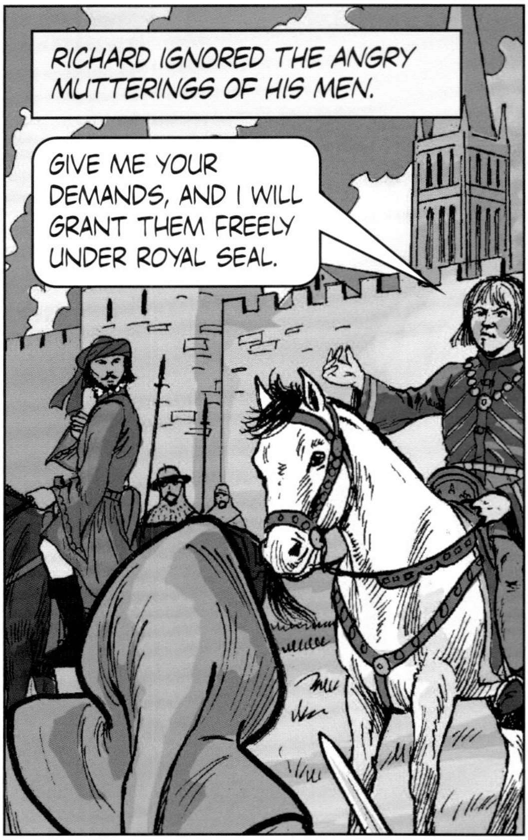
RICHARD IGNORED THE ANGRY MUTTERINGS OF HIS MEN.
GIVE ME YOUR DEMANDS, AND I WILL GRANT THEM FREELY UNDER ROYAL SEAL.

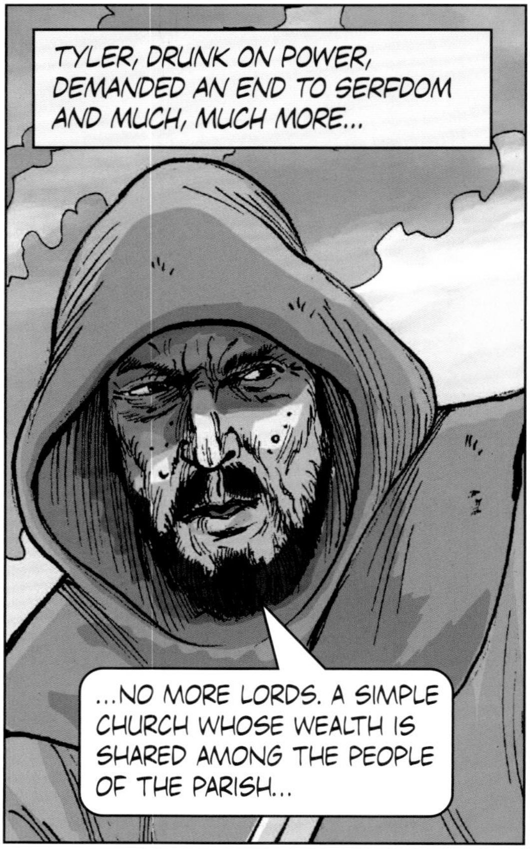
TYLER, DRUNK ON POWER, DEMANDED AN END TO SERFDOM AND MUCH, MUCH MORE...
...NO MORE LORDS. A SIMPLE CHURCH WHOSE WEALTH IS SHARED AMONG THE PEOPLE OF THE PARISH...

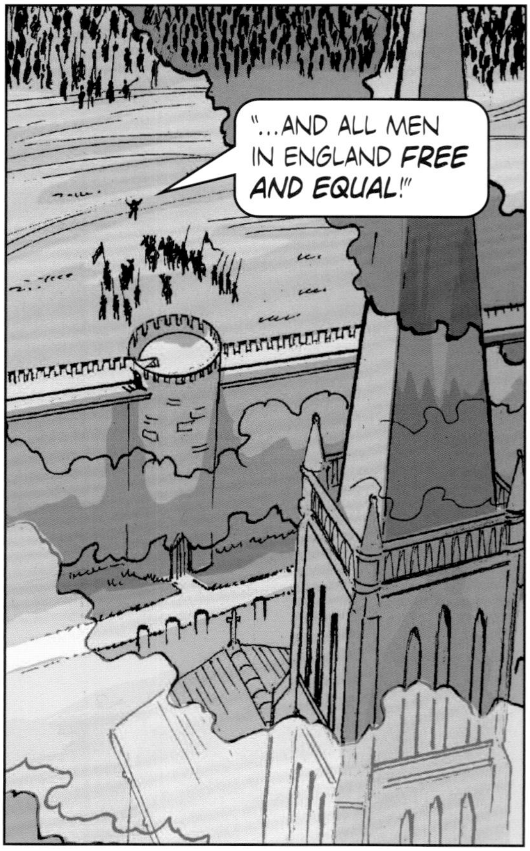
"...AND ALL MEN IN ENGLAND **FREE AND EQUAL**!"

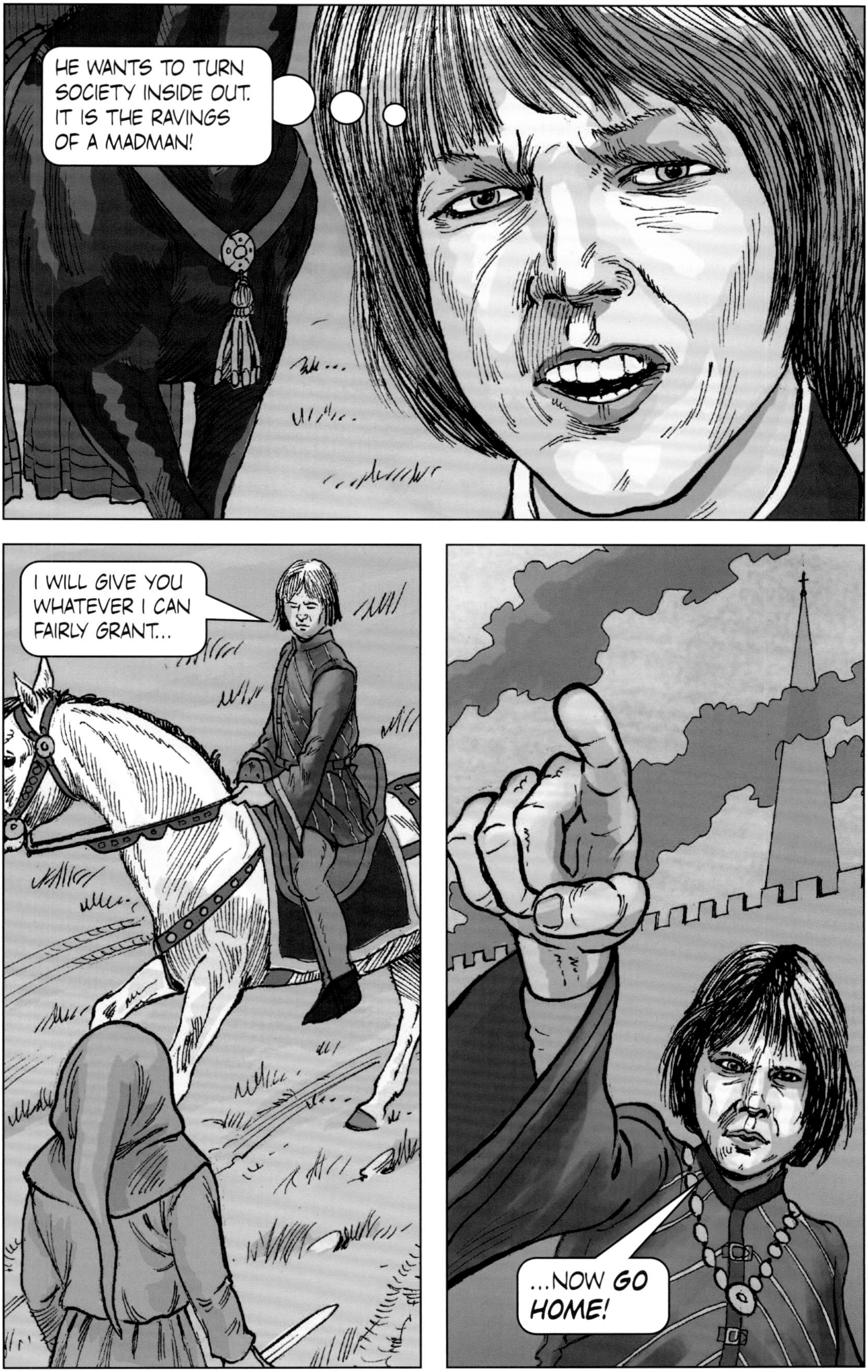
HE WANTS TO TURN SOCIETY INSIDE OUT. IT IS THE RAVINGS OF A MADMAN!
I WILL GIVE YOU WHATEVER I CAN FAIRLY GRANT...
...NOW GO HOME!

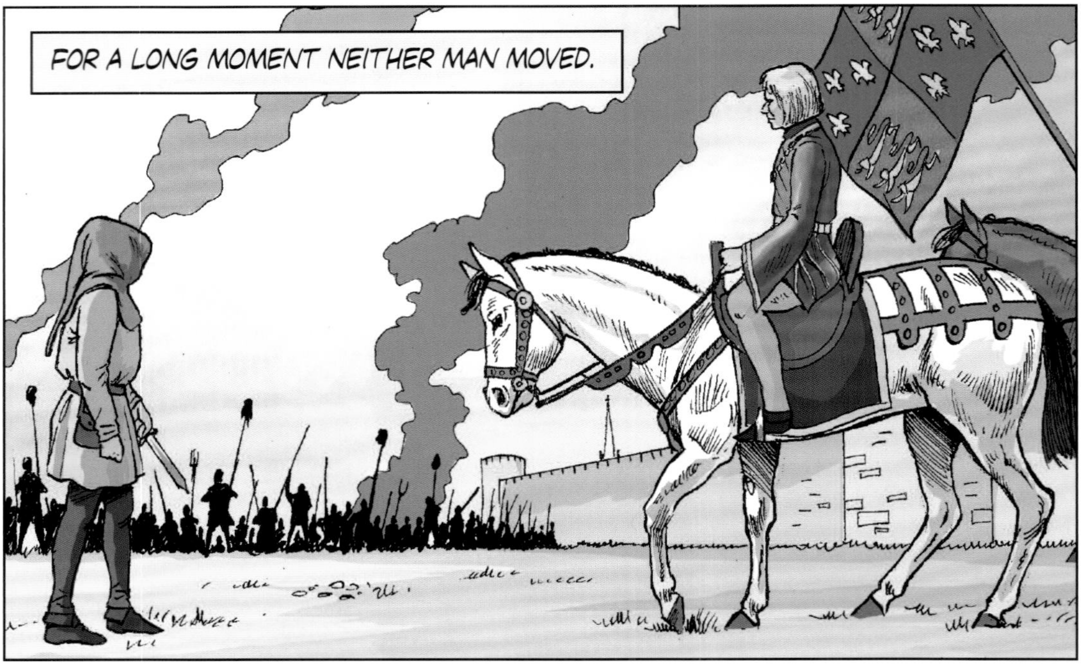
FOR A LONG MOMENT NEITHER MAN MOVED.

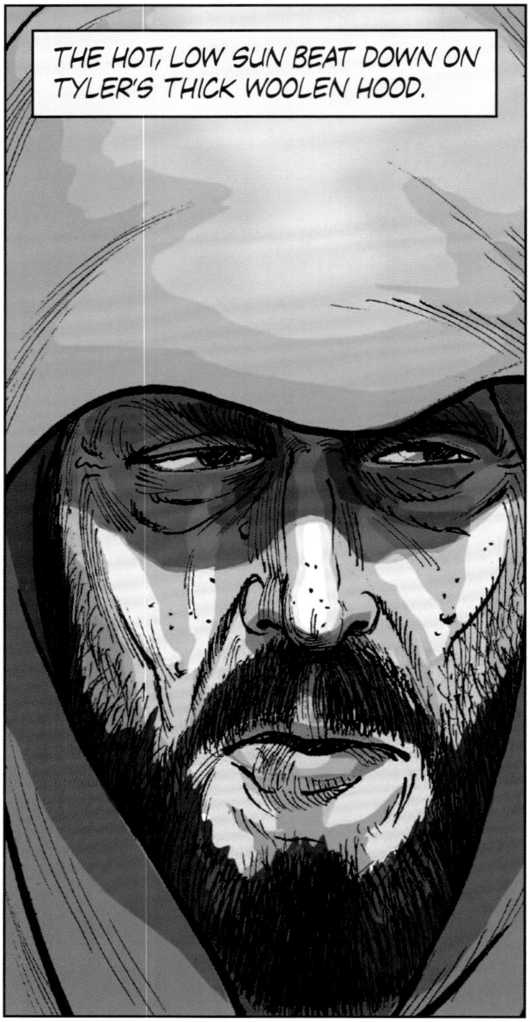
THE HOT, LOW SUN BEAT DOWN ON TYLER'S THICK WOOLEN HOOD.

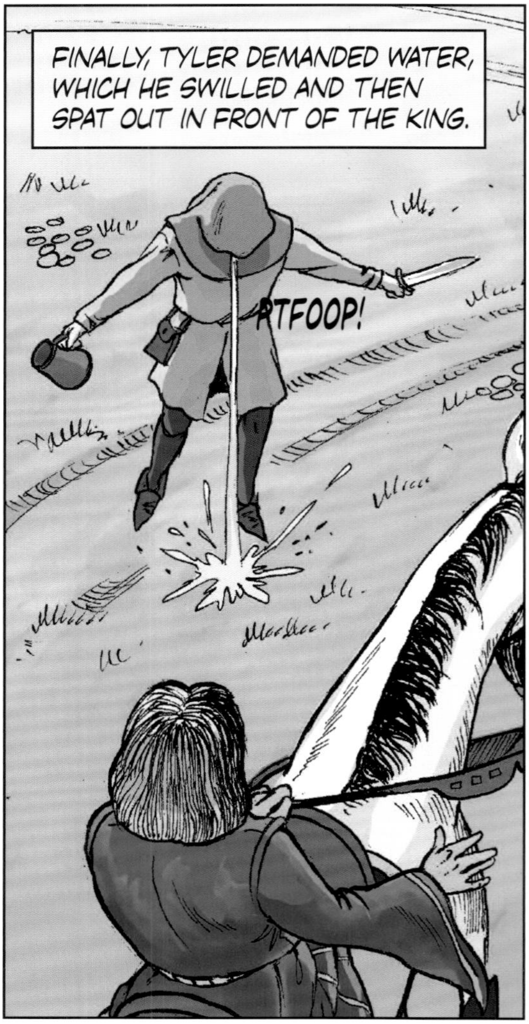
FINALLY, TYLER DEMANDED WATER, WHICH HE SWILLED AND THEN SPAT OUT IN FRONT OF THE KING.
PTFOOP!

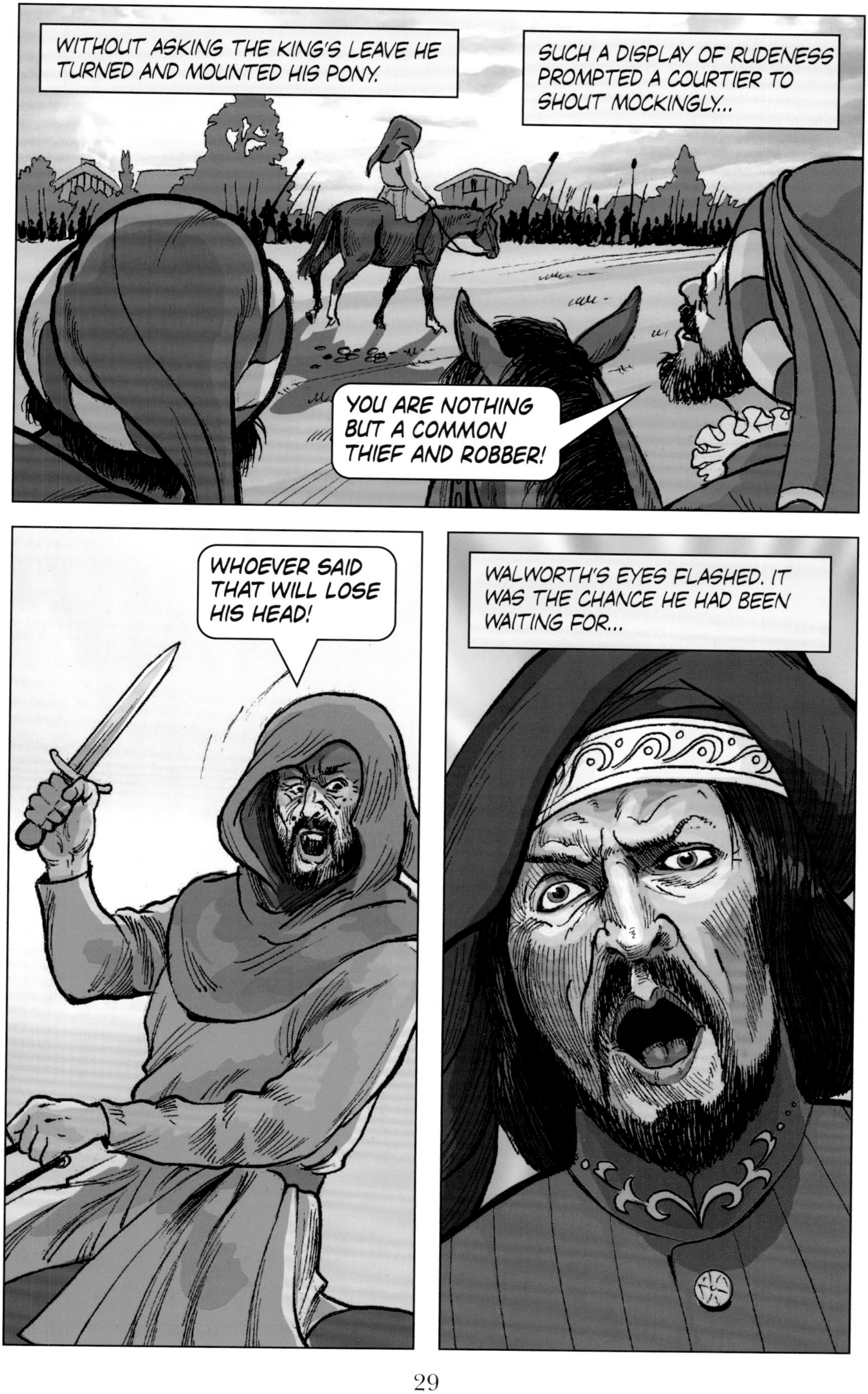

WITHOUT ASKING THE KING'S LEAVE HE TURNED AND MOUNTED HIS PONY.
SUCH A DISPLAY OF RUDENESS PROMPTED A COURTIER TO SHOUT MOCKINGLY...
YOU ARE NOTHING BUT A COMMON THIEF AND ROBBER!
WHOEVER SAID THAT WILL LOSE HIS HEAD!
WALWORTH'S EYES FLASHED. IT WAS THE CHANCE HE HAD BEEN WAITING FOR...

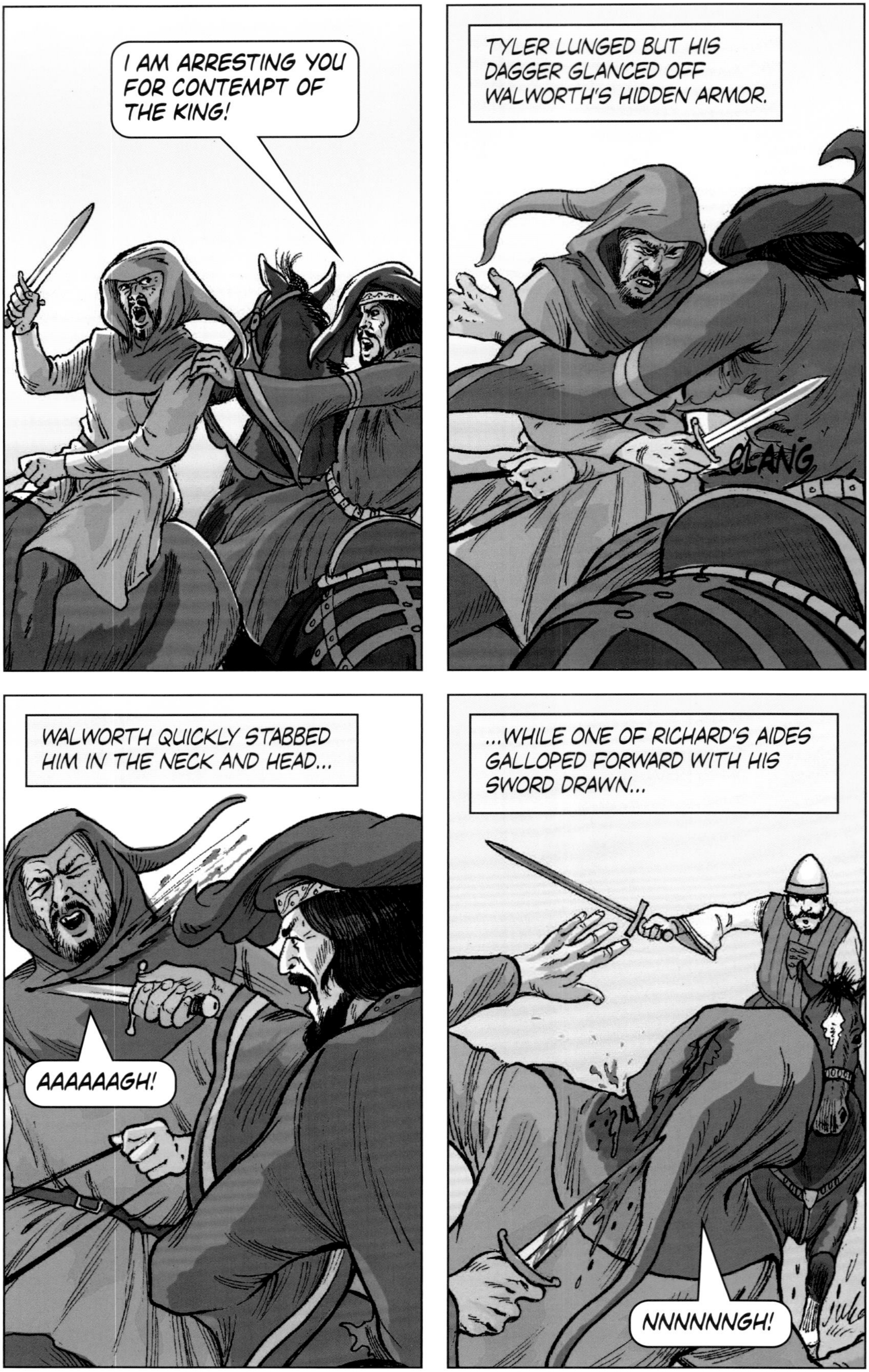
I AM ARRESTING YOU FOR CONTEMPT OF THE KING!
TYLER LUNGED BUT HIS DAGGER GLANCED OFF WALWORTH'S HIDDEN ARMOR.
CLANG
WALWORTH QUICKLY STABBED HIM IN THE NECK AND HEAD...
AAAAAAGH!
...WHILE ONE OF RICHARD'S AIDES GALLOPED FORWARD WITH HIS SWORD DRAWN...
NNNNNNGH!

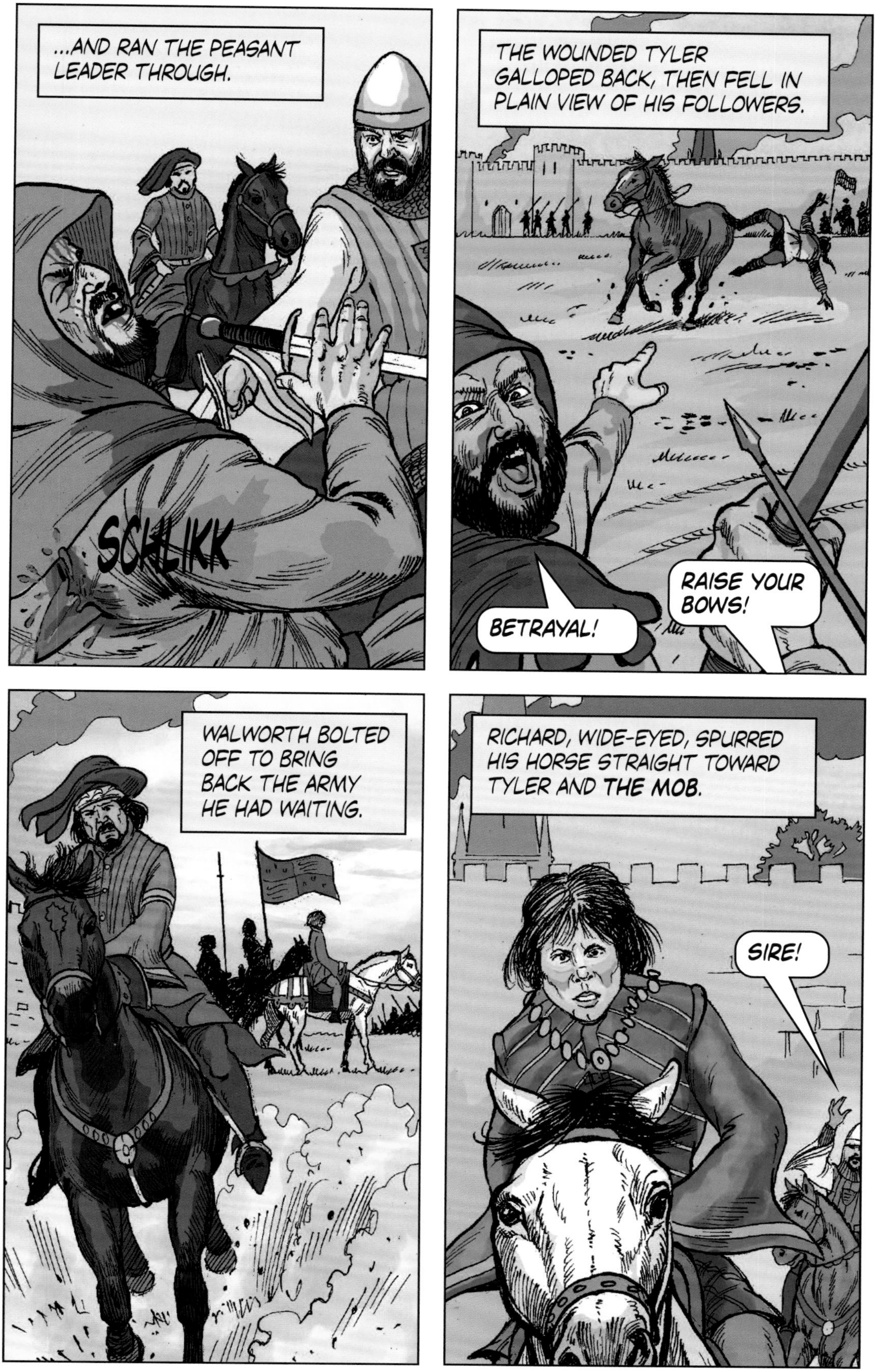
...AND RAN THE PEASANT LEADER THROUGH.
SCHLIKK
THE WOUNDED TYLER GALLOPED BACK, THEN FELL IN PLAIN VIEW OF HIS FOLLOWERS.
BETRAYAL!
RAISE YOUR BOWS!
WALWORTH BOLTED OFF TO BRING BACK THE ARMY HE HAD WAITING.
RICHARD, WIDE-EYED, SPURRED HIS HORSE STRAIGHT TOWARD TYLER AND THE MOB.
SIRE!

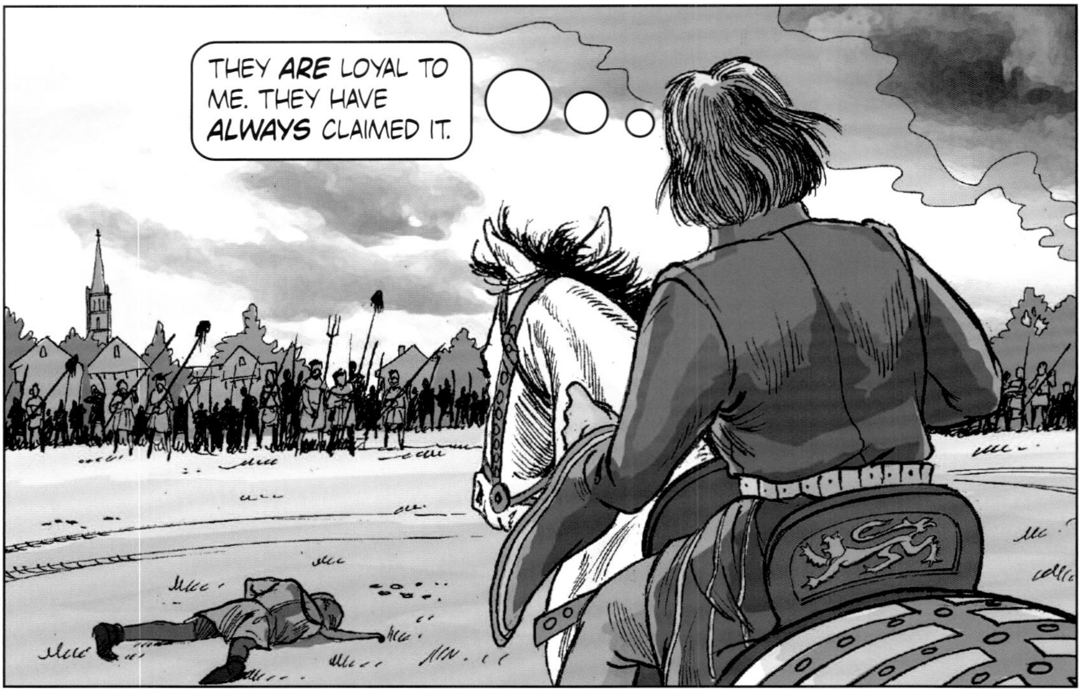
THEY ARE LOYAL TO ME. THEY HAVE ALWAYS CLAIMED IT.

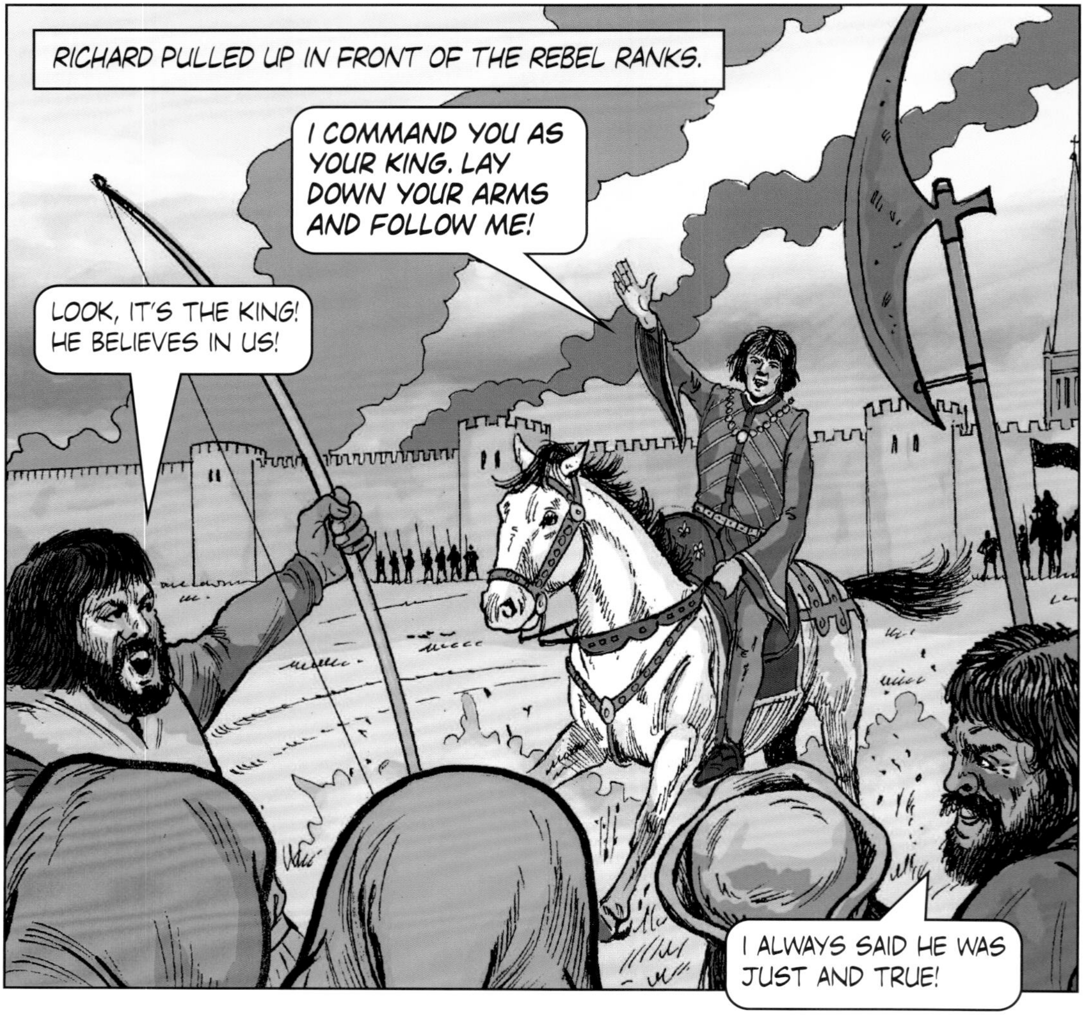
RICHARD PULLED UP IN FRONT OF THE REBEL RANKS.
I COMMAND YOU AS YOUR KING. LAY DOWN YOUR ARMS AND FOLLOW ME!
LOOK, IT'S THE KING! HE BELIEVES IN US!
I ALWAYS SAID HE WAS JUST AND TRUE!

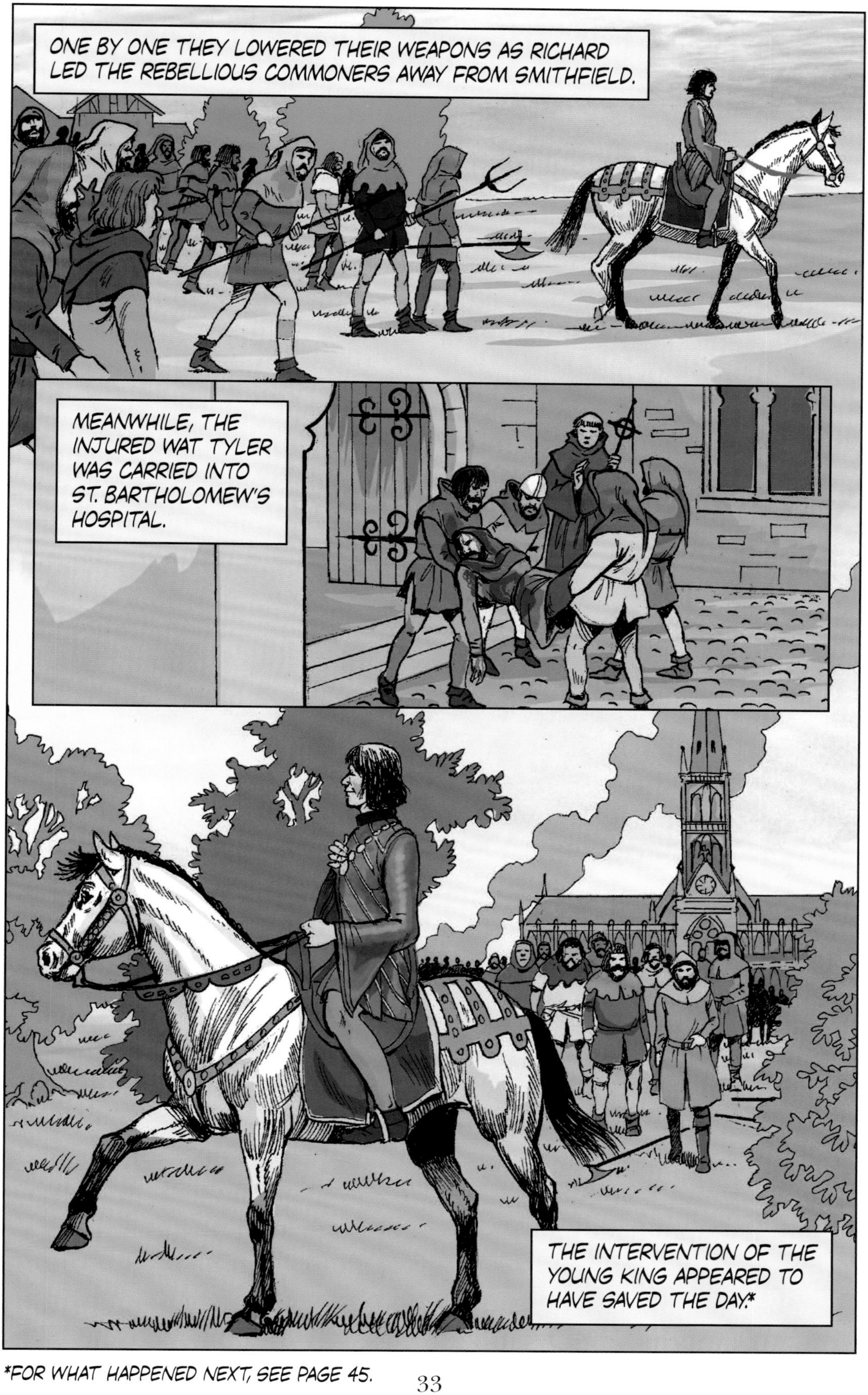
ONE BY ONE THEY LOWERED THEIR WEAPONS AS RICHARD LED THE REBELLIOUS COMMONERS AWAY FROM SMITHFIELD.
MEANWHILE, THE INJURED WAT TYLER WAS CARRIED INTO ST. BARTHOLOMEW'S HOSPITAL.
THE INTERVENTION OF THE YOUNG KING APPEARED TO HAVE SAVED THE DAY.*

*FOR WHAT HAPPENED NEXT, SEE PAGE 45.

The Battle of Bryn Glas
The Revolt of Owain Glyndwr

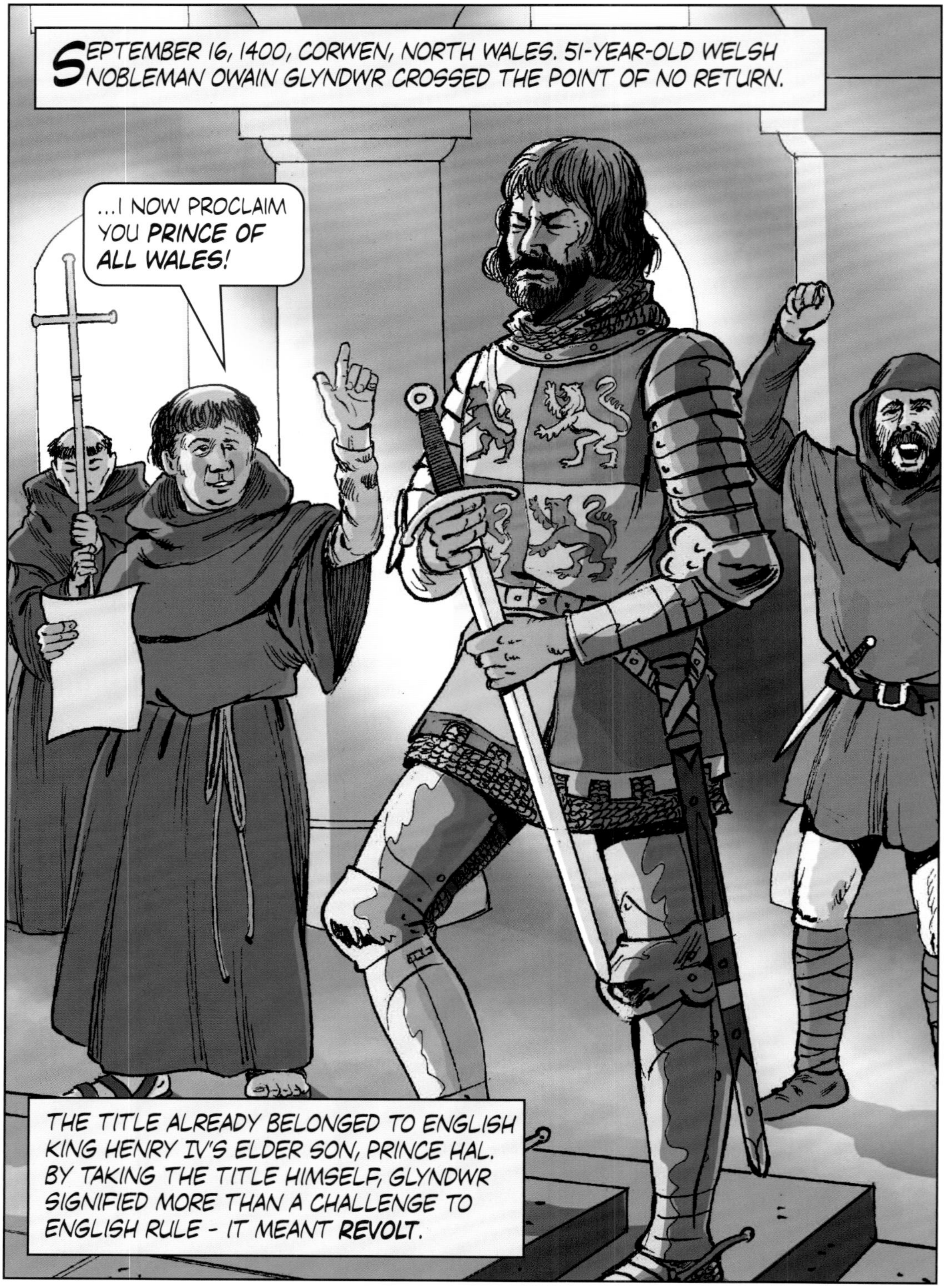
SEPTEMBER 16, 1400, CORWEN, NORTH WALES. 51-YEAR-OLD WELSH NOBLEMAN OWAIN GLYNDWR CROSSED THE POINT OF NO RETURN.
...I NOW PROCLAIM YOU **PRINCE OF ALL WALES!**
THE TITLE ALREADY BELONGED TO ENGLISH KING HENRY IV'S ELDER SON, PRINCE HAL. BY TAKING THE TITLE HIMSELF, GLYNDWR SIGNIFIED MORE THAN A CHALLENGE TO ENGLISH RULE - IT MEANT **REVOLT**.

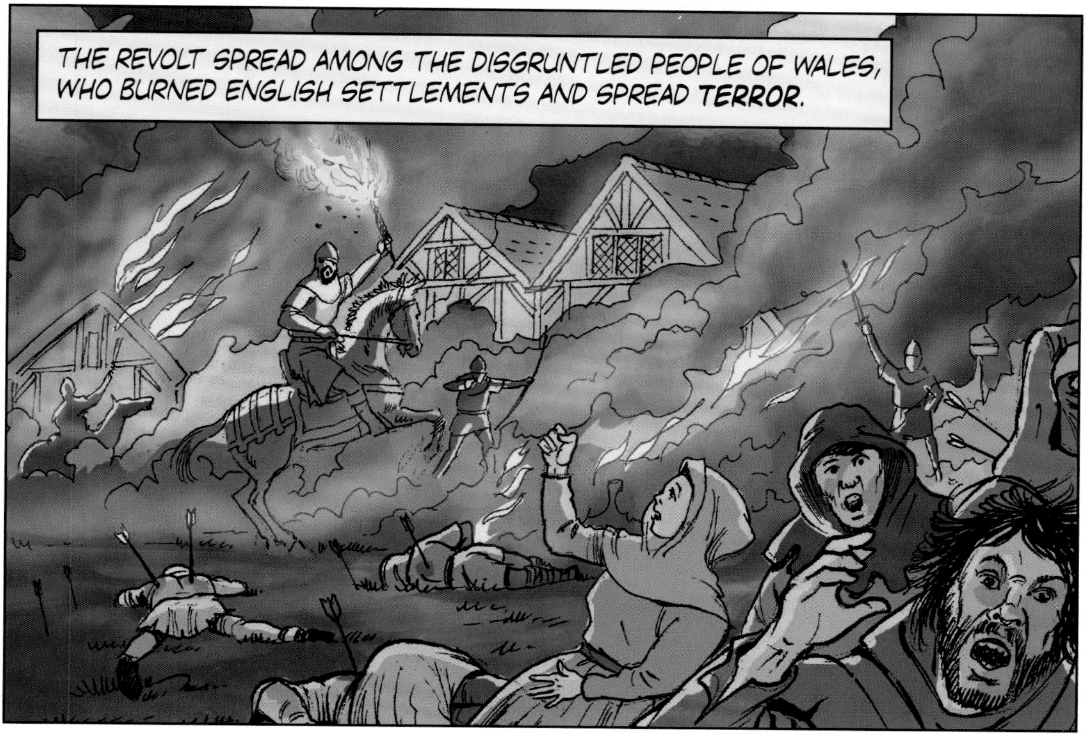
THE REVOLT SPREAD AMONG THE DISGRUNTLED PEOPLE OF WALES, WHO BURNED ENGLISH SETTLEMENTS AND SPREAD **TERROR**.

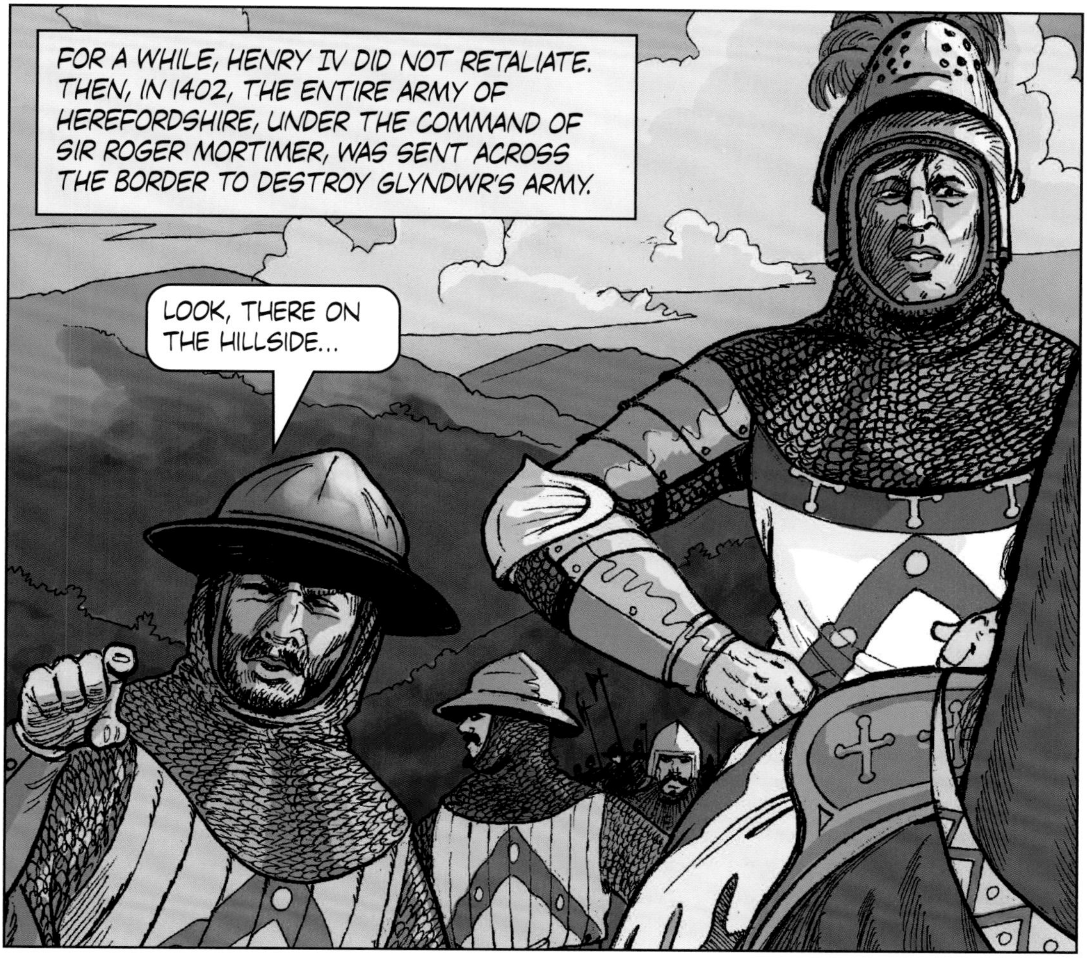
FOR A WHILE, HENRY IV DID NOT RETALIATE. THEN, IN 1402, THE ENTIRE ARMY OF HEREFORDSHIRE, UNDER THE COMMAND OF SIR ROGER MORTIMER, WAS SENT ACROSS THE BORDER TO DESTROY GLYNDWR'S ARMY.
LOOK, THERE ON THE HILLSIDE...

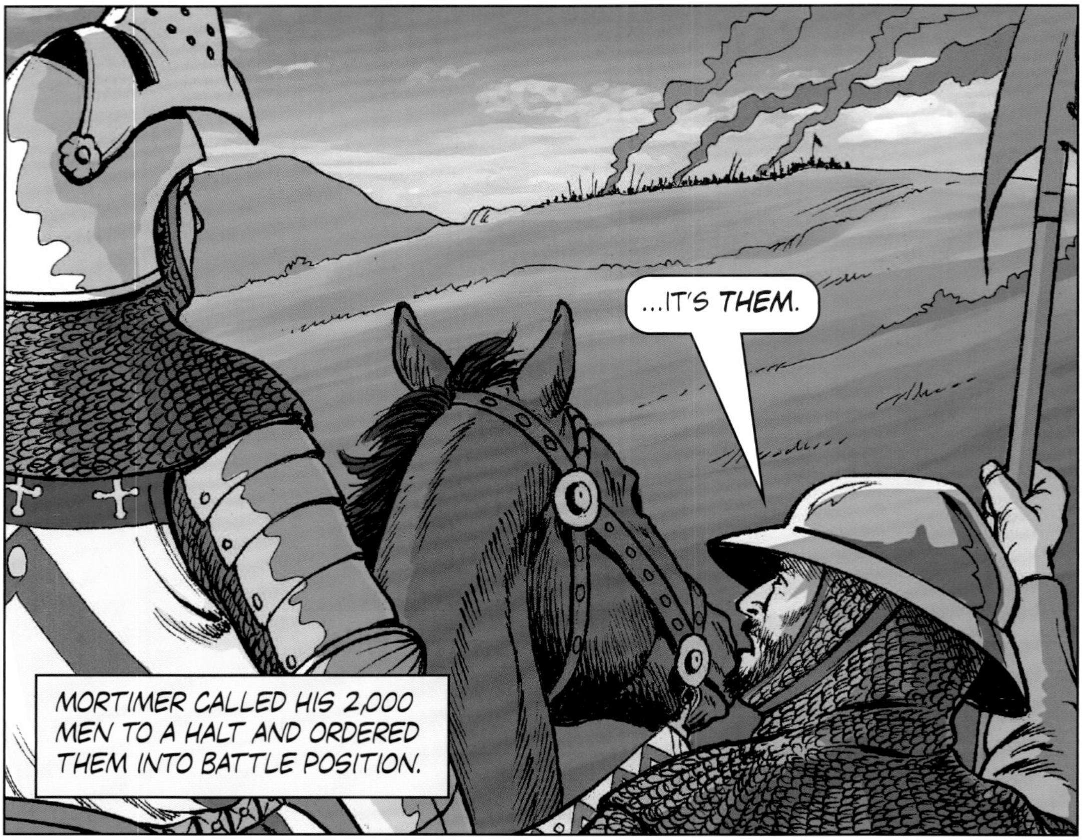
...IT'S THEM.
MORTIMER CALLED HIS 2,000 MEN TO A HALT AND ORDERED THEM INTO BATTLE POSITION.

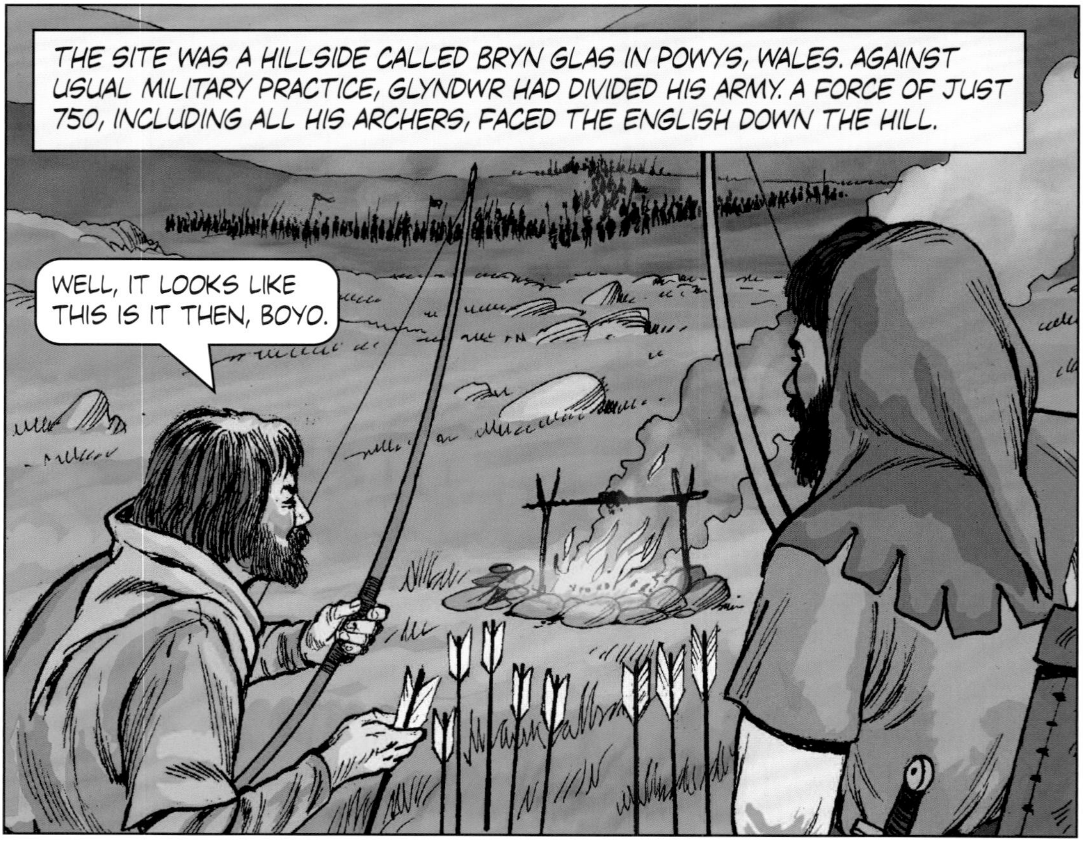
THE SITE WAS A HILLSIDE CALLED BRYN GLAS IN POWYS, WALES. AGAINST USUAL MILITARY PRACTICE, GLYNDWR HAD DIVIDED HIS ARMY. A FORCE OF JUST 750, INCLUDING ALL HIS ARCHERS, FACED THE ENGLISH DOWN THE HILL.
WELL, IT LOOKS LIKE THIS IS IT THEN, BOYO.

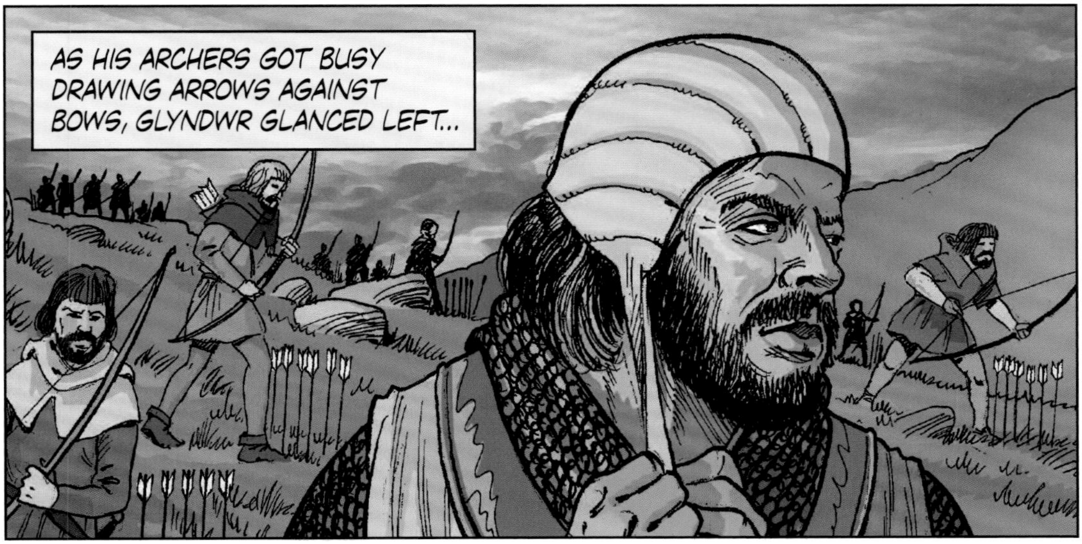
AS HIS ARCHERS GOT BUSY DRAWING ARROWS AGAINST BOWS, GLYNDWR GLANCED LEFT...

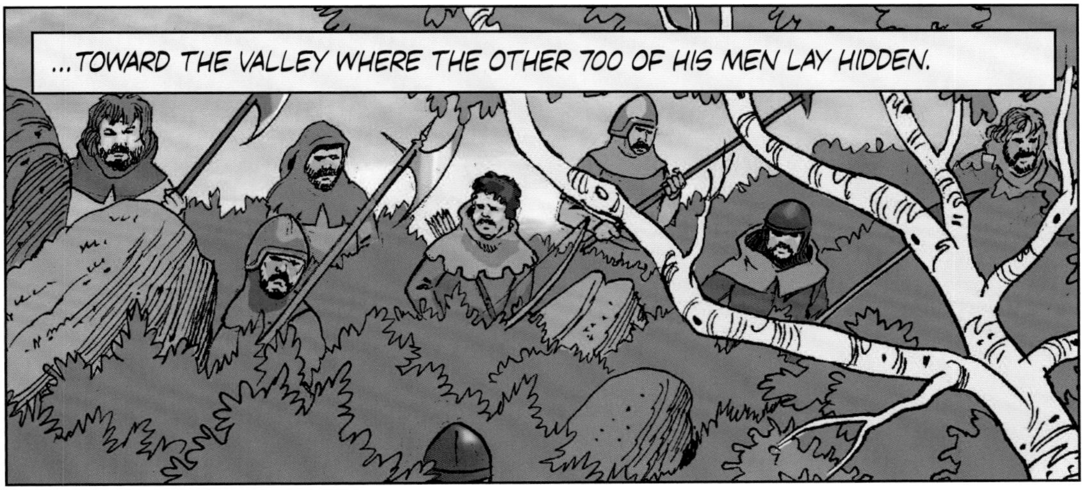
...TOWARD THE VALLEY WHERE THE OTHER 700 OF HIS MEN LAY HIDDEN.

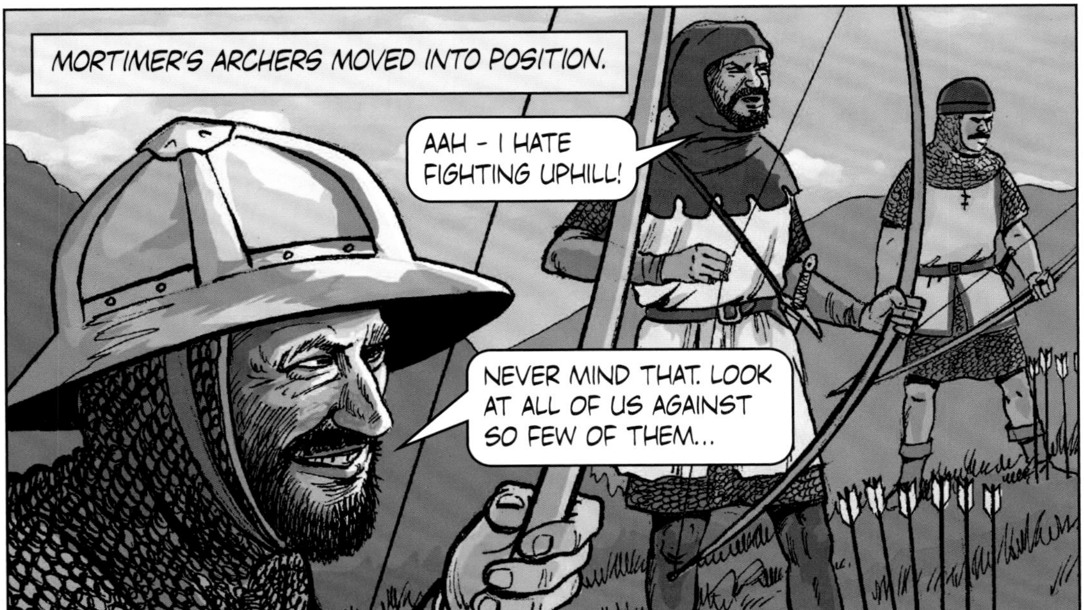
MORTIMER'S ARCHERS MOVED INTO POSITION.
AAH - I HATE FIGHTING UPHILL!
NEVER MIND THAT. LOOK AT ALL OF US AGAINST SO FEW OF THEM...

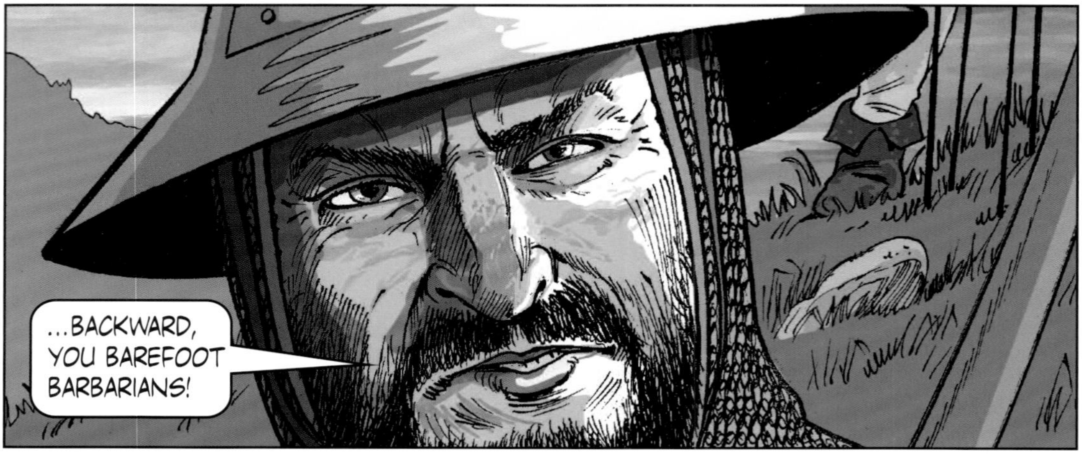
...BACKWARD, YOU BAREFOOT BARBARIANS!

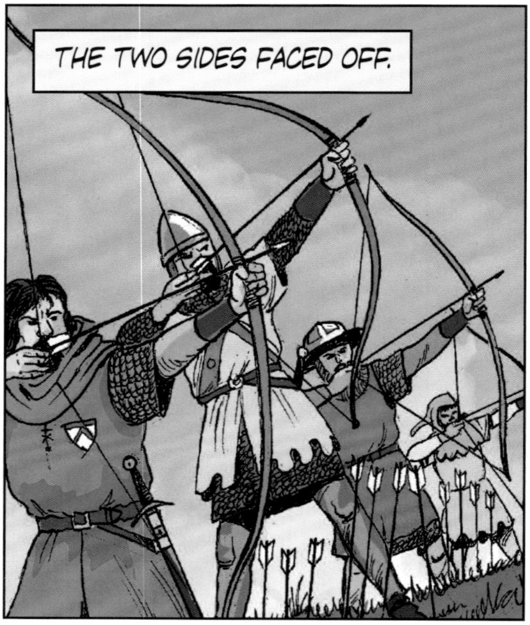
THE TWO SIDES FACED OFF.

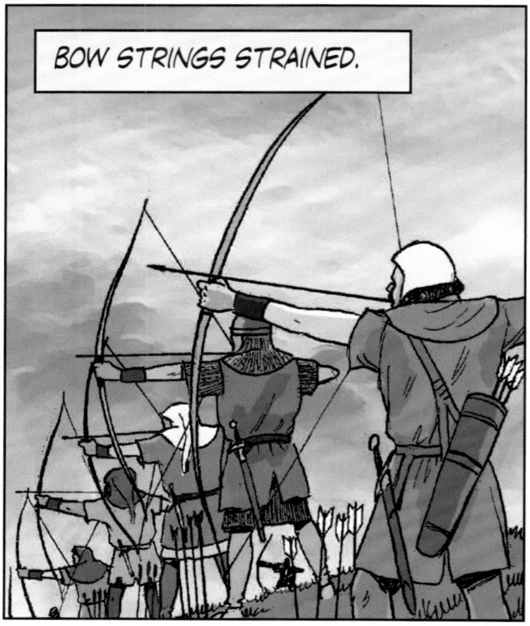
BOW STRINGS STRAINED.

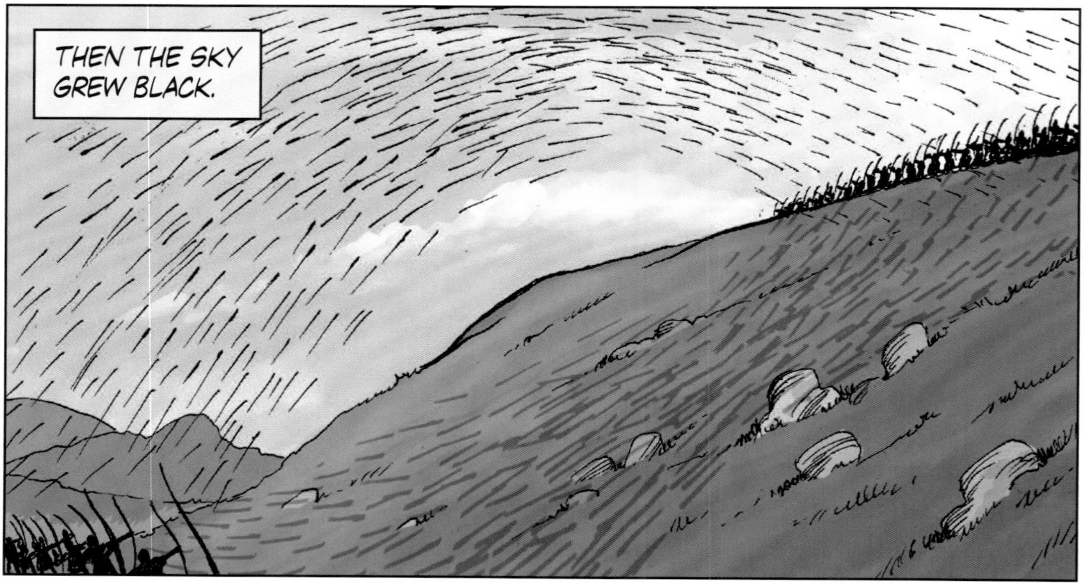
THEN THE SKY GREW BLACK.

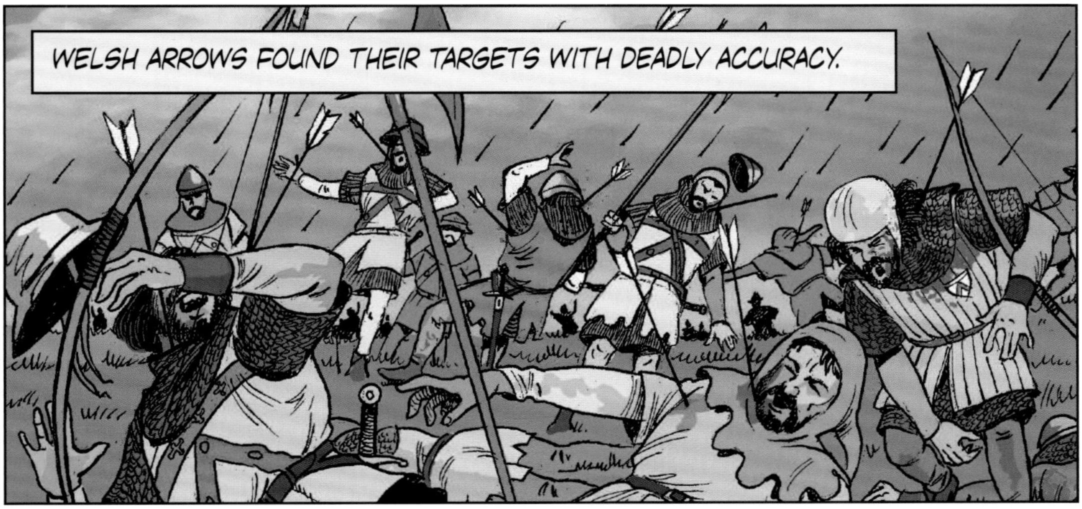
WELSH ARROWS FOUND THEIR TARGETS WITH DEADLY ACCURACY.

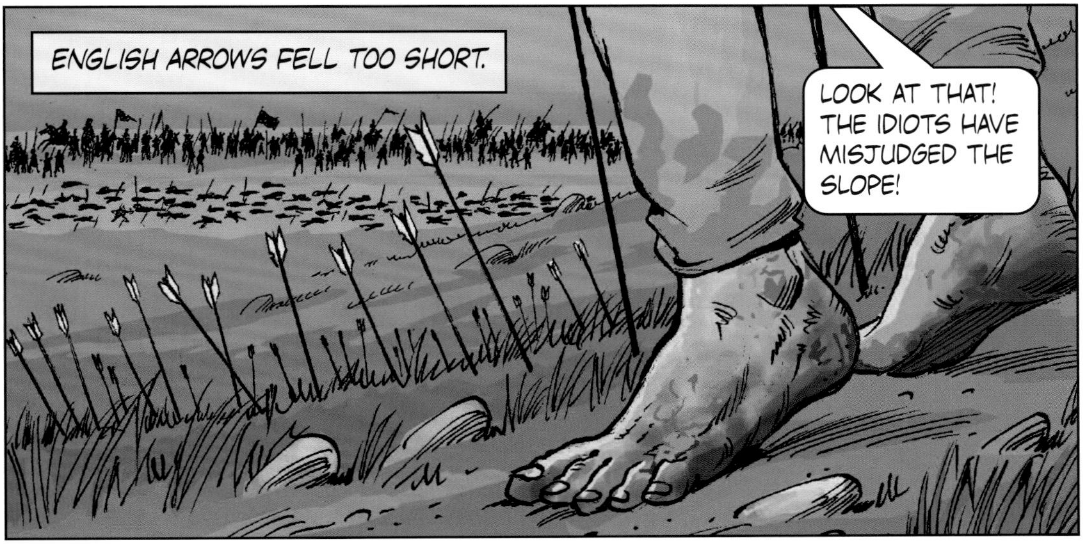
ENGLISH ARROWS FELL TOO SHORT.
LOOK AT THAT! THE IDIOTS HAVE MISJUDGED THE SLOPE!

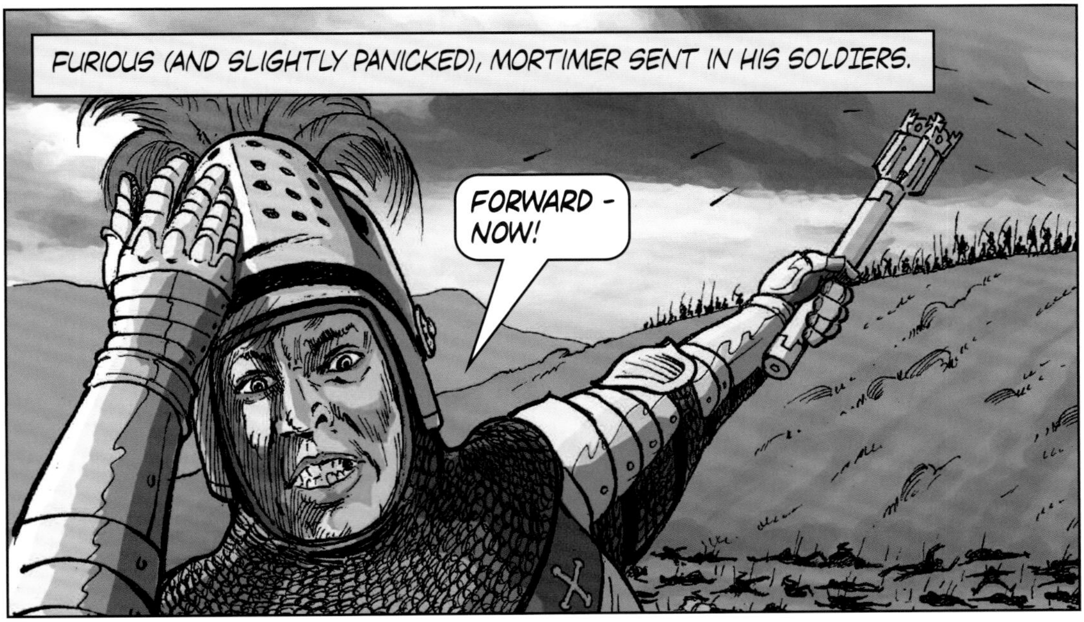
FURIOUS (AND SLIGHTLY PANICKED), MORTIMER SENT IN HIS SOLDIERS.
FORWARD - NOW!

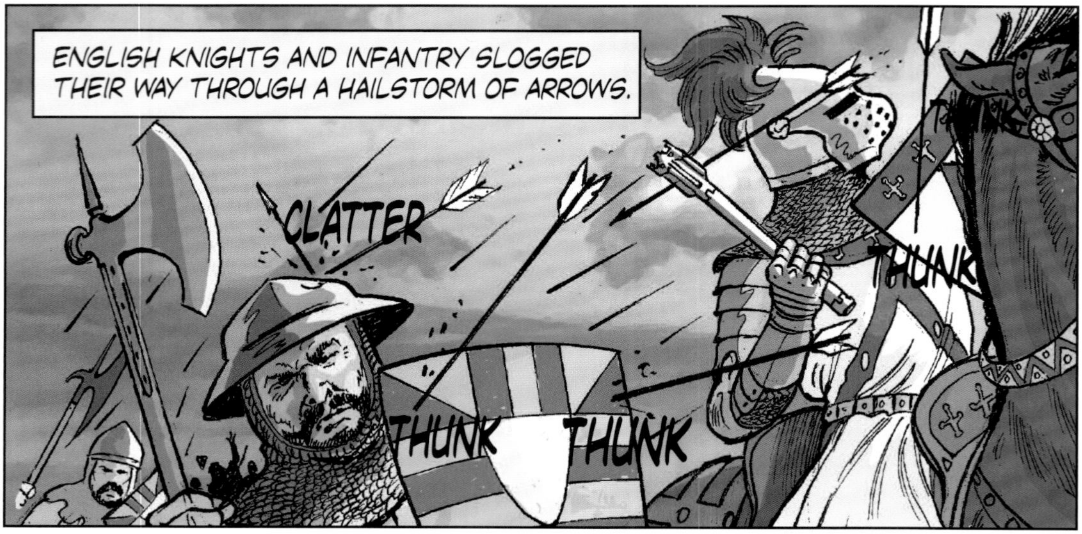
ENGLISH KNIGHTS AND INFANTRY SLOGGED THEIR WAY THROUGH A HAILSTORM OF ARROWS.
CLATTER
THUNK
THUNK
THUNK
THUNK

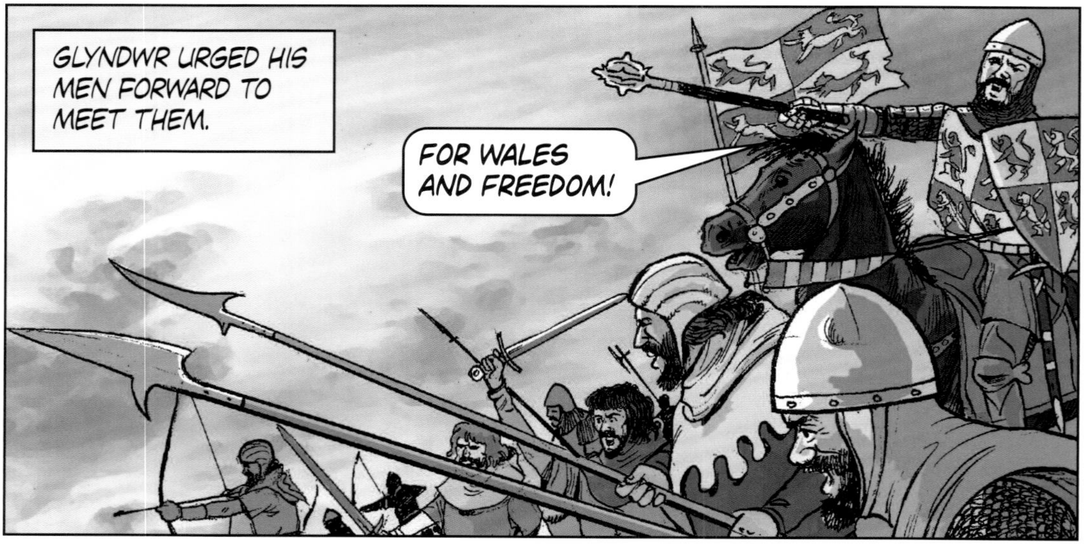
GLYNDWR URGED HIS MEN FORWARD TO MEET THEM.
FOR WALES AND FREEDOM!

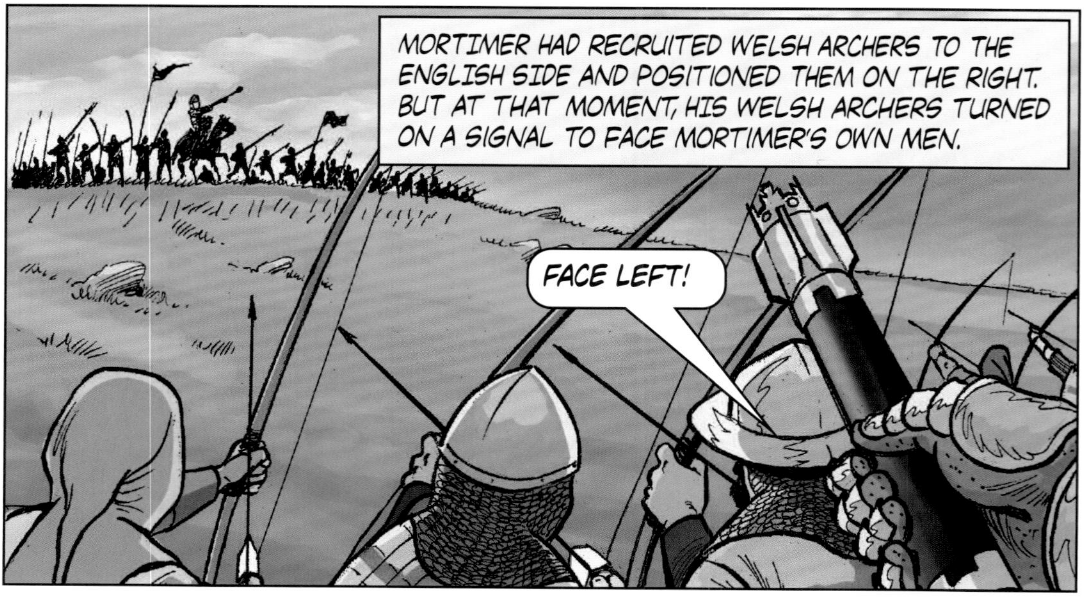
MORTIMER HAD RECRUITED WELSH ARCHERS TO THE ENGLISH SIDE AND POSITIONED THEM ON THE RIGHT. BUT AT THAT MOMENT, HIS WELSH ARCHERS TURNED ON A SIGNAL TO FACE MORTIMER'S OWN MEN.
FACE LEFT!

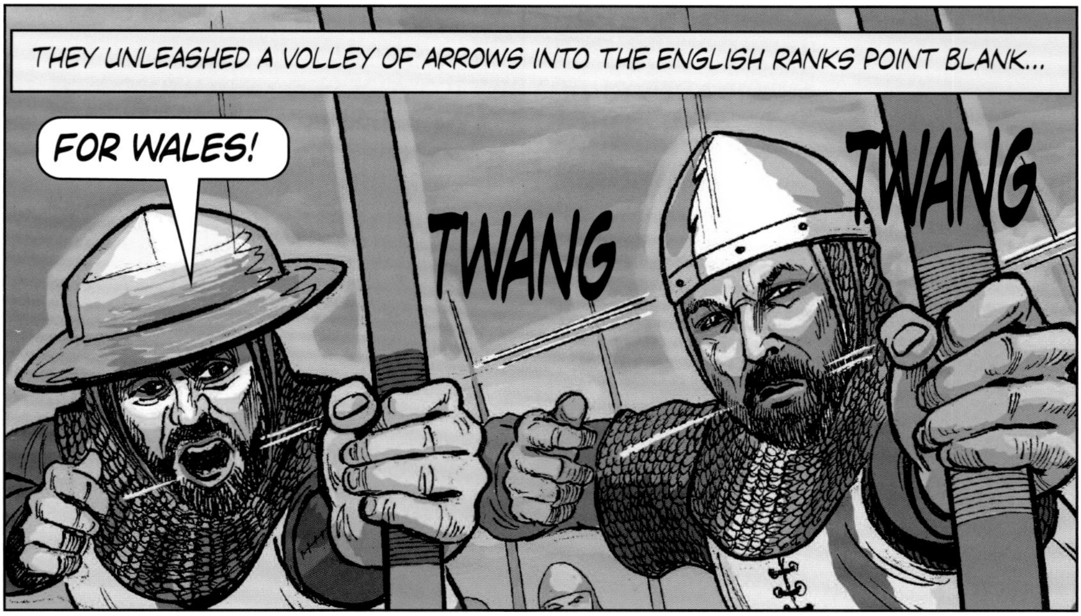
THEY UNLEASHED A VOLLEY OF ARROWS INTO THE ENGLISH RANKS POINT BLANK...
FOR WALES!
TWANG
TWANG

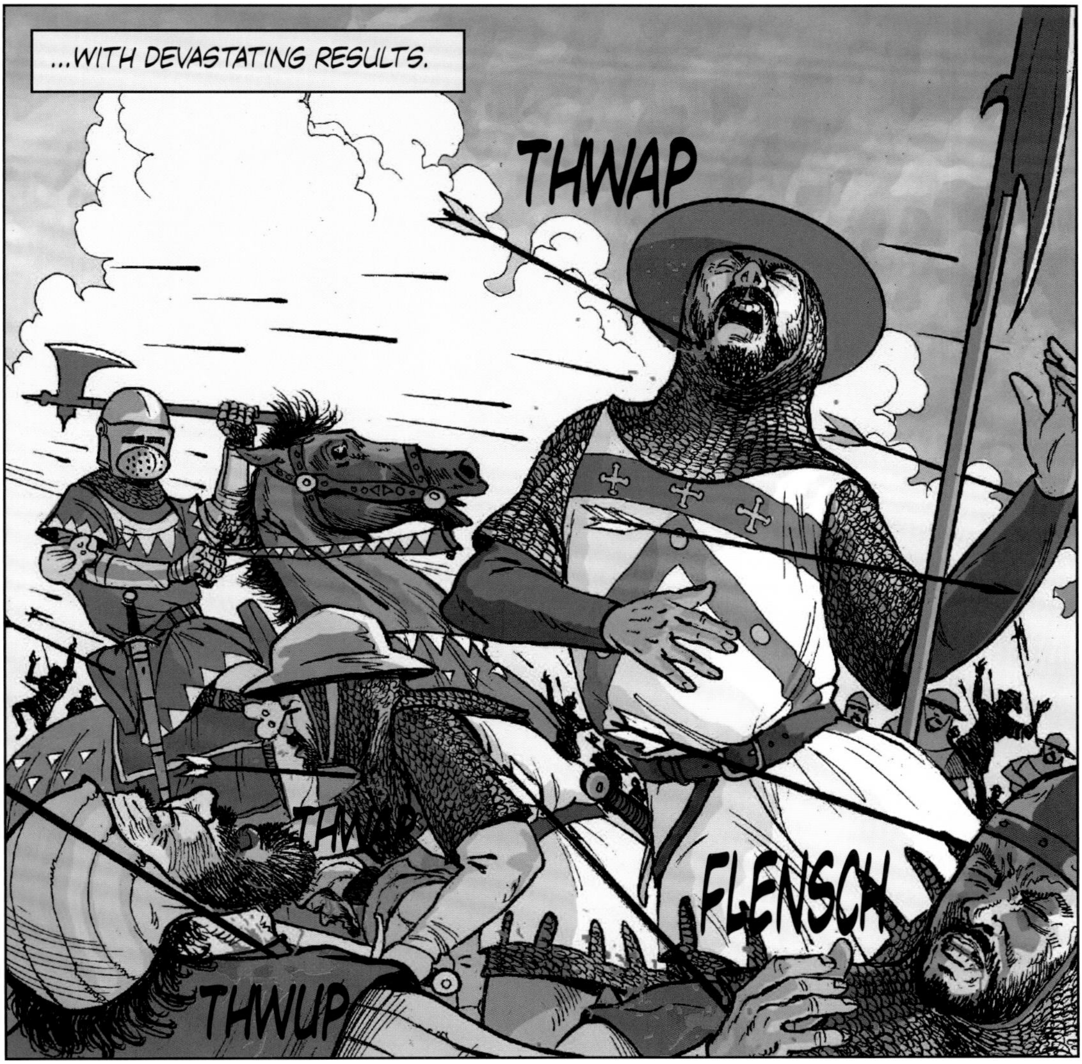
...WITH DEVASTATING RESULTS.
THWAP
FLENSCH
THWUP

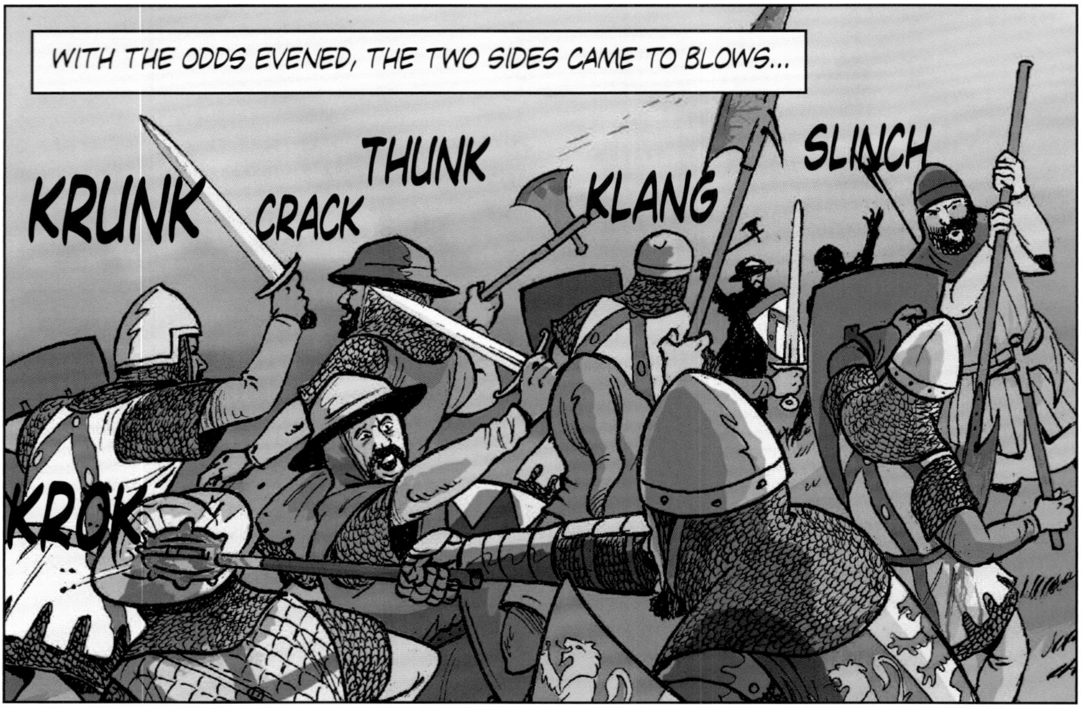
WITH THE ODDS EVENED, THE TWO SIDES CAME TO BLOWS...
KRUNK
CRACK
THUNK
KLANG
SLINCH
KROK

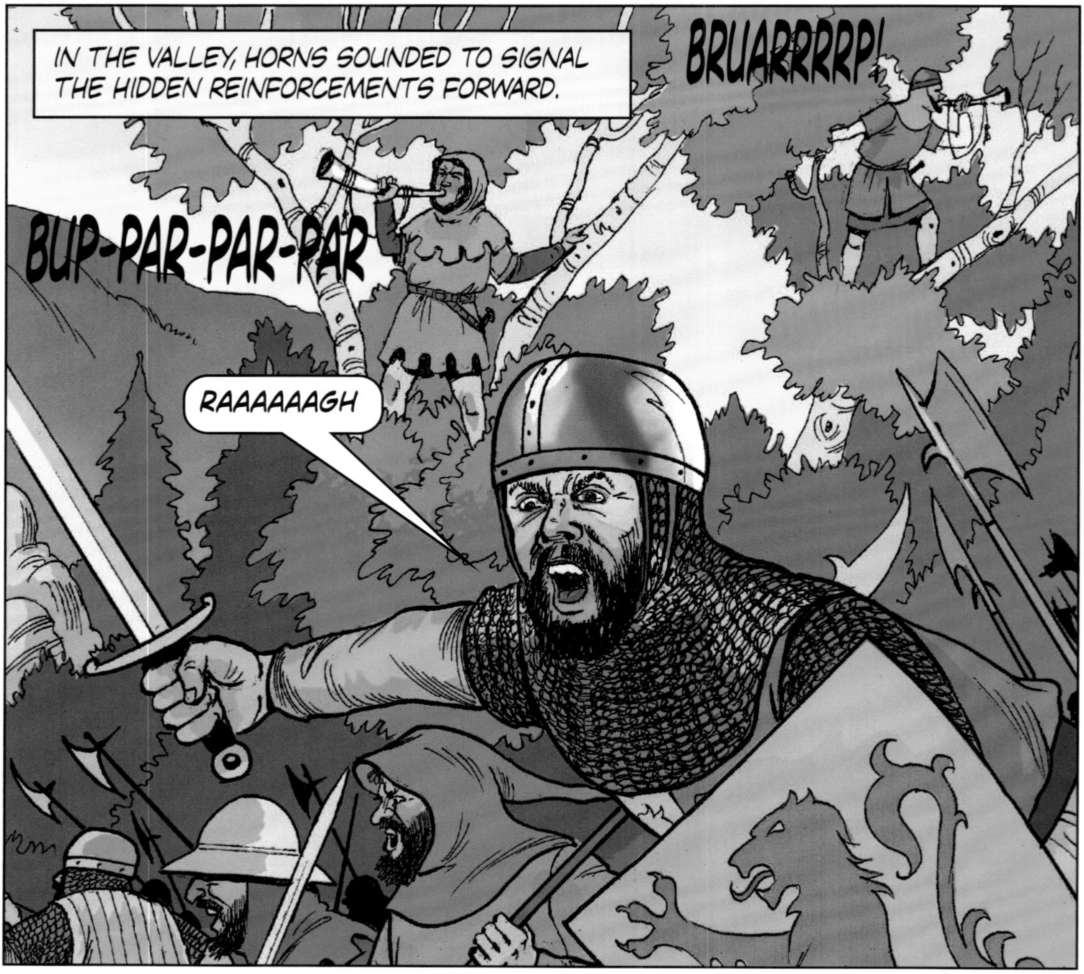
IN THE VALLEY, HORNS SOUNDED TO SIGNAL THE HIDDEN REINFORCEMENTS FORWARD.
BRUARRRRP!
BUP-PAR-PAR-PAR
RAAAAAAGH

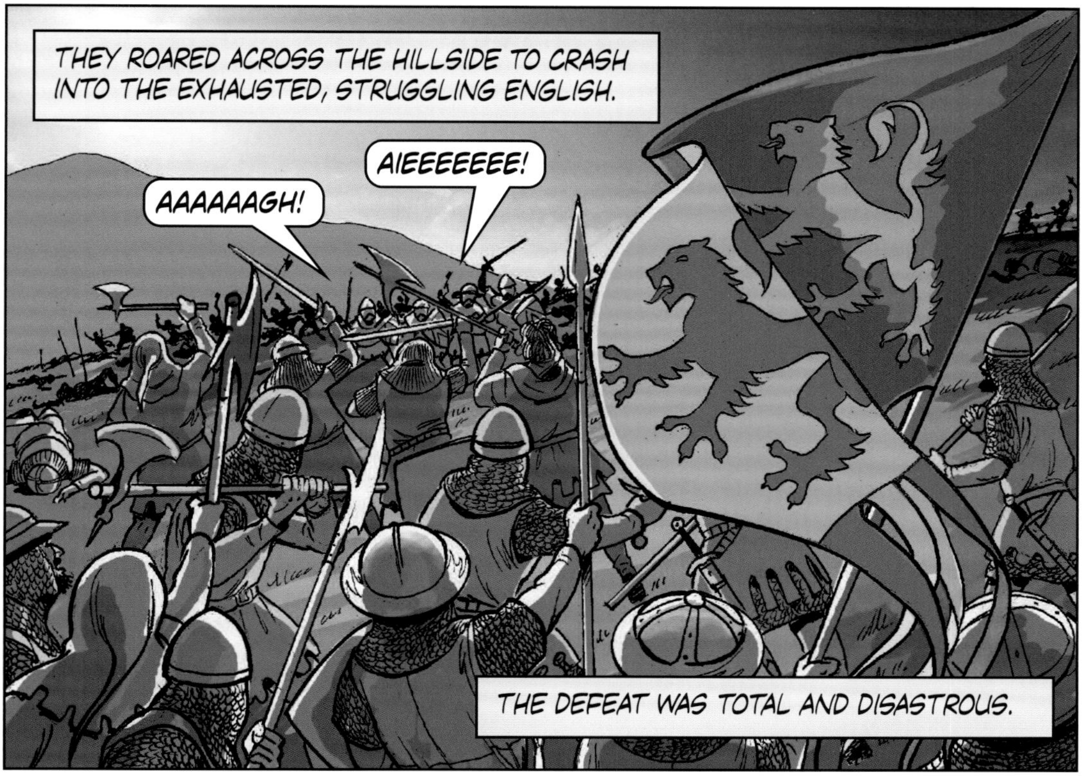
THEY ROARED ACROSS THE HILLSIDE TO CRASH INTO THE EXHAUSTED, STRUGGLING ENGLISH.
AAAAAAGH!
AIEEEEEEE!
THE DEFEAT WAS TOTAL AND DISASTROUS.

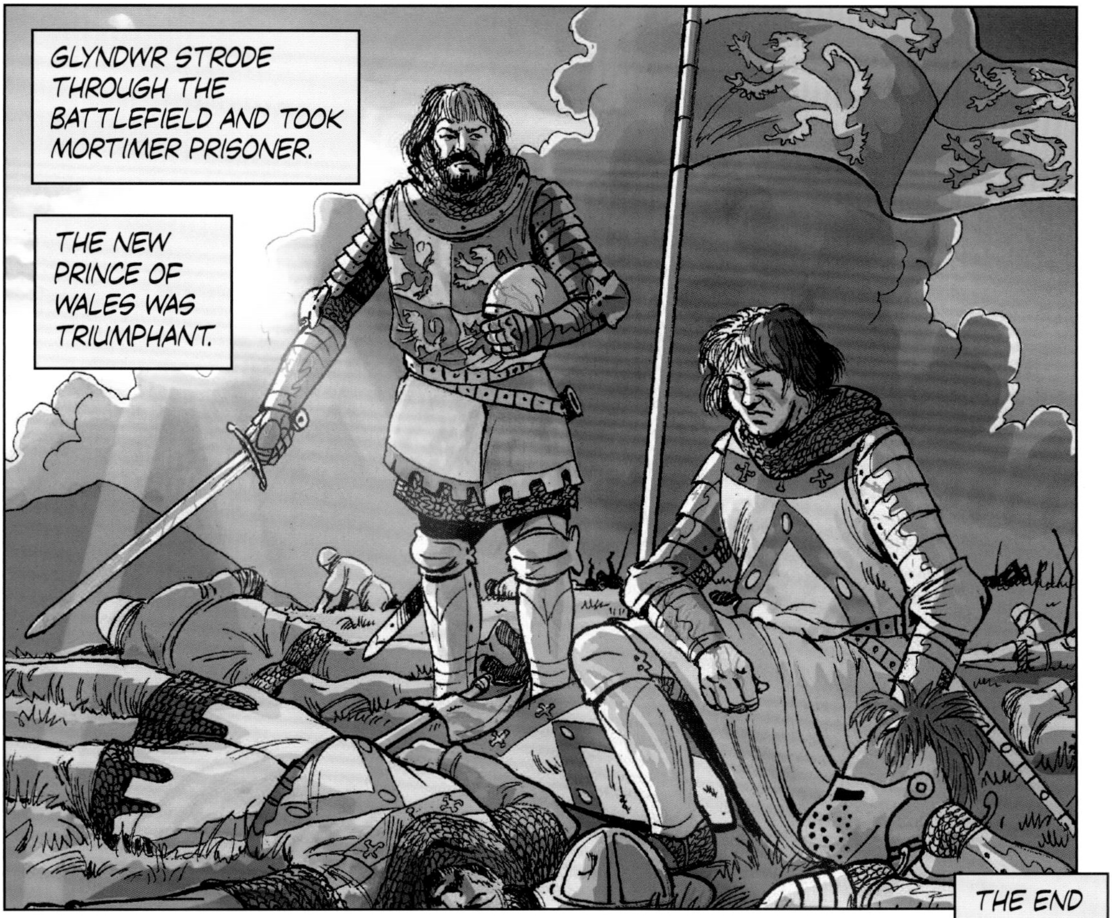
GLYNDWR STRODE THROUGH THE BATTLEFIELD AND TOOK MORTIMER PRISONER.
THE NEW PRINCE OF WALES WAS TRIUMPHANT.
THE END

Scotland's Last Stand

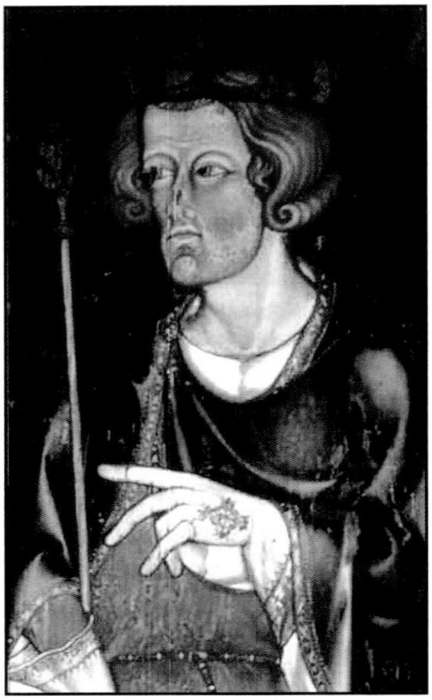

Edward I personally led the second invasion of Scotland.

After the battle at Stirling Bridge, Wallace and Moray became joint Guardians of Scotland, acting in the name of their deposed king, John Balliol. Moray died of his wounds soon after. In the meantime, Edward I had begun raising an army to invade once more and finally end the rebellion.

A Rebel's Downfall

As Edward's forces entered the lowlands, Wallace was content to sit back and follow their movements. He knew the land would not supply the English soldiers with the food they needed, and he intended to wait and attack them guerilla-style when they retreated. By the time they reached central Scotland, Edward's men were starving and mutinous. When his scouts spotted Wallace's army near Falkirk, however, Edward hurried his men forward forcing Wallace into battle.

The result was total defeat for the Scots, mainly by a devastating new weapon—the English longbow. Wallace fled the battlefield and soon gave up the Guardianship of Scotland. In 1305, he was betrayed, captured, tried for treason, and gruesomely executed in London.

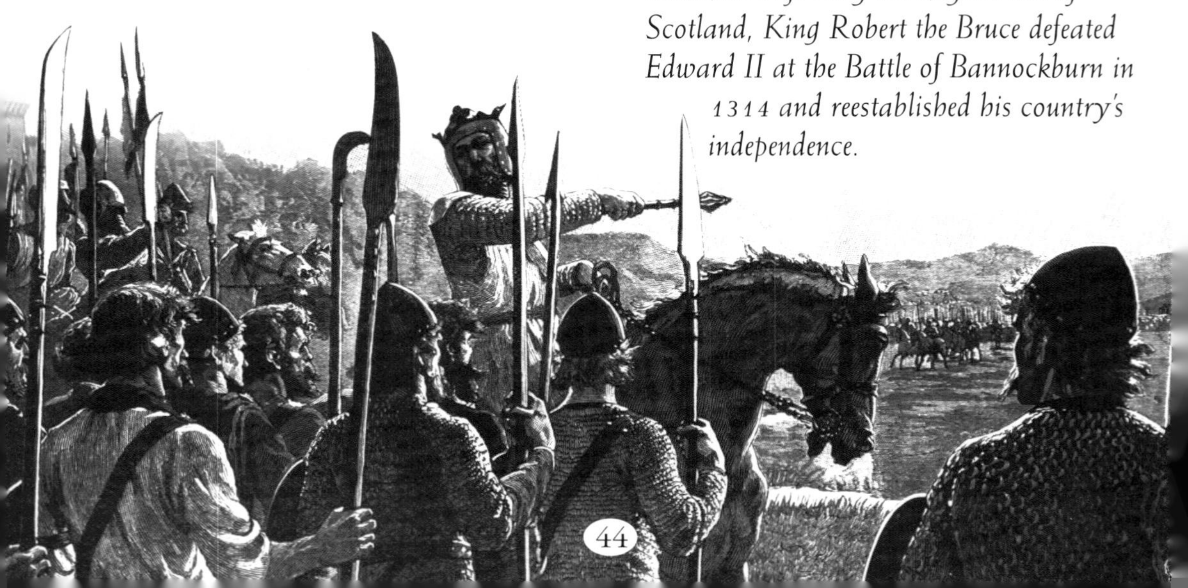

Eventually, after an eight-year campaign dedicated to forcing the English out of Scotland, King Robert the Bruce defeated Edward II at the Battle of Bannockburn in 1314 and reestablished his country's independence.

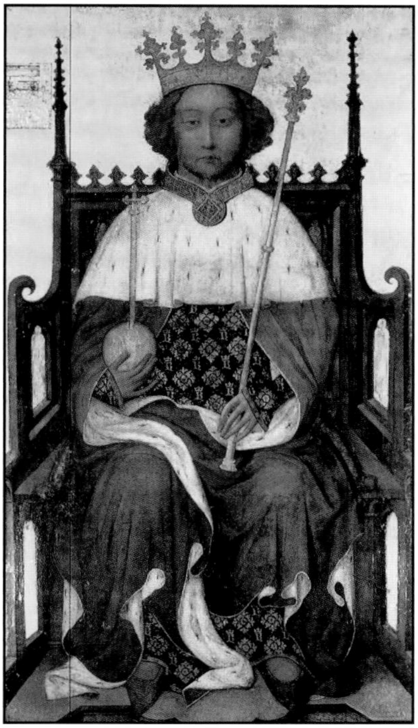

Richard II's fear turned to fury when the realm became safe.

A King's Justice

In 1381 in London, Walworth returned with his militia to find Smithfield deserted. The wounded Wat Tyler was dragged from St. Bartholomew's Hospital and beheaded. When Walworth caught up with Richard, the king had him kneel and knighted him.

The king's men captured and killed the revolt's ringleaders. Gibbets, or gallows, sprang up across the land to fulfill the angry king's demand for executions. Yet the grievances of the people remained. Richard addressed their protests with these words: "Rustics you were, and rustics you are still. You will remain in bondage, not as before, but incomparably harsher." The poll tax was scrapped, but the revolution had failed.

An Icon of Wales

In 1402, Owain Glyndwr had captured his enemy, Reynold de Grey, and traded him for a large ransom from King Henry IV. When he tried to ransom Mortimer, Henry refused. So Glyndwr joined the Welsh. The following year the revolt spread all across Wales. In 1404, Glyndwr called his first parliament in Machynlleth and was crowned Prince of Wales. He formed an alliance with the French. England was under pressure at its borders and in battle in France. But Henry IV's armies were strong. The revolt slowly failed, and the English reclaimed Wales. Glyndwr's wife and daughters were taken prisoner in 1409, and Glyndwr disappeared, a hunted guerilla leader, into the mists of legend...

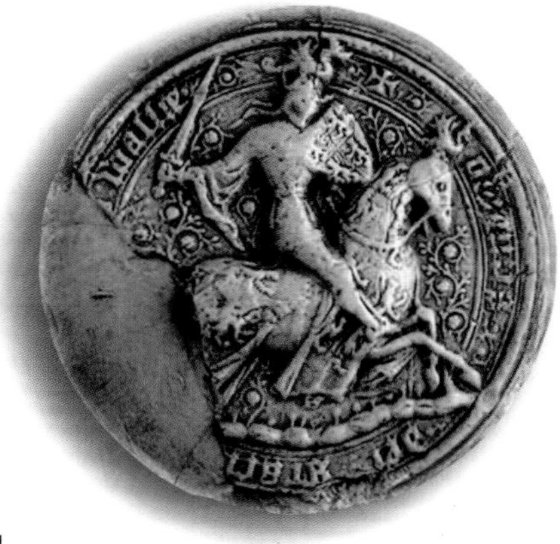

The seal of Owain Glyndwr

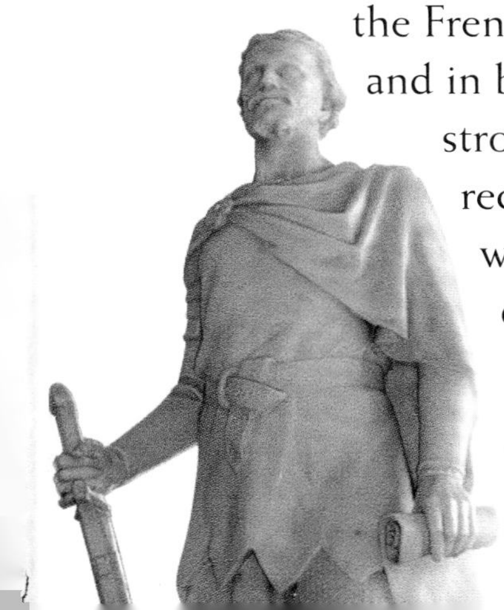

Never captured, Glyndwr remains an enduring symbol of Welsh independence to this day.

Glossary

abdicated When a monarch has given up his or her throne

avenge To take vengeance

Barbarians A derisory term used to describe people who were seen as uncultured and not members of a great civilization

boyo Welsh slang for pal or buddy

Celts A group of peoples living in Europe and Asia Minor who were driven westward by Roman and later Germanic occupation

charter A written grant where rights and privileges are defined

commoners People who are not of noble rank

contempt Disrespect or disobedience

courtier A person who attends royal court

curtsied A formal greeting, usually made by women, made by bending the knees with one foot in front of the other

discord Disagreement between people

ford A shallow part of a body of water

friar A member of certain religious orders of men

gibbets Structures with an upright post with an arm from which people are hanged by the neck with a rope; also called gallows

guerrilla A small group of combatants, such as armed civilians, using military tactics, including ambushing, sabotage, and raids to fight a larger traditional army

heirs People legally entitled to the property or rank of another on that person's death

longbow A long, hand-drawn bow that can be over six feet long

lowborn Born to a lower class in society

mayor The elected head of a city or town

mutinous Refusing to obey the orders of a person in charge

noble Belonging by rank, title or birth to the aristocracy (the upper classes) of a society or civilization

parish The members of a church

Picts A group of late Iron Age and Early Medieval Celtic people living in ancient eastern and northern Scotland

poll tax A tax levied on every adult, where both poor and rich pay the same amount

rabble A group of people thought of as being ignorant and hard to control

ransacking Going through a place, stealing, and causing damage

ransom A sum of money or other payment demanded or paid for the release of a prisoner

Royal seal An image of a king or queen impressed in wax, attached by ribbon or cord to documents to show the monarch's approval

rue Regret

rustic Backward and provincial

serfdom A legal system in which a serf, or laborer, works land owned by a landlord in exchange for protection

succession The action or process of inheriting a title such as king

swilled Washed or rinsed out

treason The crime of betraying one's country

treasurer A person appointed to manage the financial affairs of a company or other body such as a kingdom

The ruins of Harlech Castle, in Wales, lost by Owain Glyndwr to the English in 1409.

Index